Behind the Curtains

with

THE VOLCANOS
"Storm Warning"

and

The Grammy Award Winning

TRAMMPS
"Disco Inferno"

By Stephen C. Kelly

Published by:

FriesenPress
Suite 300 – 852 Fort Street
Victoria, BC, Canada V8W 1H8

www.friesenpress.com

Distributed to the trade by The Ingram Book Company

Table of Contents

Introduction

To make the biography relaxing to read, the author has written it in laymen's terms. Other authors have written novels on what they believe to be the truth about The Volcanos and The Trammps, However, those authors didn't travel with The Volcanos or The Trammps, and surely they were not members of the groups in question. Their versions of what took place during each group's tenure are strictly fiction. The facts in this biography are strictly that—the facts. As a member and organizer of The Volcanos, I am the most qualified person to bring you the true story. What I plan to depict is how reckless, harsh, cold blooded, and underhanded some entertainers can be when climbing the ladder of success.

The contents of this biography are not intended to demean, harm, insult, defame, embarrass, or disrespect the individuals mentioned in it. The sole reason for writing this biography is to inform the reader of how The Volcanos and The Trammps endured pleasure, disappointment, hell, and a unique method of back-stabbing among their members, the groups' managers and record companies. The book is a triumph, not only for its author, but also for the members of The Volcanos and The Trammps.

In the end, the book in your hands will have taken you through the amazing world of show business. Hopefully when you turn the page, the curtain will rise, and the show will begin.

Enjoy!

THE VOLCANOS

Harold "Doc" Wade, Stephen Kelly, Stanley Wade

Eugene Jones

Acknowledgments

Our Lord and Savior, Jesus Christ, who blessed me and guided me through this biography.

Gwendolyn J. Kelly, my wife, thanks for your comforting support during the writing of this biography. *Kimberly Railey,* my special niece and my guardian angel. *Linaida Rivera-Cervantes,* my guide child, a very special person in my life, love always. *Norman Harris,* an elegant guitar player, songwriter, studio musician, arranger and producer from Philly. He's gone, but not forgotten. *Ronnie Baker,* a magnificent bass guitar player, studio musician, songwriter and producer from Philly. He's gone, but not forgotten. *Larry Washington,* an outstanding percussionist and studio musician from Philly. He's gone, but not forgotten. *Frank Virtue,* many thanks to Frank and his family for the use of Virtue's Recording Studio. He's gone, but not forgotten. *Georgie Woods,* a man with a heart of gold. Thanks for the air play and the bookings at the Uptown Theater. He's gone, and will never be forgotten. *Weldon Arthur McDougal III,* what can I say, a man who believed in himself and others. Thanks for the guidance and support. He's gone, but he will never be forgotten. *Sam D'Amico,* if it wasn't for Sam I would probably still be playing drums. Thanks for the guidance and the name Prettyboy for my record label. He's gone, and is truly missed.

Luther Randolph, one of Harthon's three musketeers, arranger, pianist, and organist. *Johnny Stiles,* another Harthon musketeer. Arranger, violinist, string arranger, and studio engineer.

William Luby, bass vocalist. Thanks Luby for being there when the group needed a bass singer. I appreciated your support. *Charles B. Kelly Sr.,* my dad. Thanks for the guidance during my childhood. We didn't always agree, but your teaching made me a better and stronger person. He's gone, and dearly missed. *Juliet Kelly,* my mom. What a beautiful woman she was. Always willing to listen, and give advice if you requested it. She was very spiritual and full of love. The years passed has not quelled my hunger for her presence. She is gone, and dearly missed by all who knew her. *Patricia Ann Kelly,* my sister. What can I say, she was the oldest and she would let you know it. She is dearly missed by the family and her children. *Charles B. Kelly Jr.,* my brother. What an artistic individual. If it could be done, he could do it. In the music industry he was known as "Turk." He was the road manager for Blue Magic, and the soundman for The Trammps. He's gone, but not forgotten. *Michael Lee Kelly,* my brother. Mike has a little rhythm in him as well. He is well-known for the particular way of playing his conga drums. A percussionist at heart. *Irvin V. Kelly,* my baby brother. I say that modestly—Irvin is taller than I. He has participated in the music industry as well. He also was the soundman and driver for The Trammps. However, his forte is fishing. *Stanley Wade, Harold Wade, and Eugene Jones,* I would like to thank these individuals for believing in me and supporting my dream, which turned into our dream. Without them the dream would not have been fulfilled. As for The Trammps, who knows: would there have been a group called The Trammps? The Volcanos is where it all began.

Jerry Blavat, how can I thank Jerry? He was the first and only jock who paid The Volcanos for a TV appearance. He played the Volcanoes records and continues to play them to this day, not overlooking his everlasting support of The Trammps. Thanks, Jerry! *Frank Lipsius,* the son of the late Harold Lipsius. Frank is well-deserving of this acknowledgement. When Frank took over Jamie/Guyden Records, his first assignment was to undo anything that might have been intentionally done or overlooked by the former owner of the company. He initiated royalty rights to The Volcanos and other recording artists. Thanks Frank! *Felix A. DiPrinzio,* here's a guy with a heart of gold. Felix and his daughter Rita have been my accountants and adviser for over twenty years. To this day, I have never encountered financial headaches in regards to my personal lifestyle, or my record company. Thanks Felix! And to the rest of my family and friends, who I acknowledge.

The Author: Stephen C. Kelly

The author, who is he? Born December 28, 1943 at St. Joseph's Hospital, Philadelphia, PA, Stephen Courtney Kelly was the fourth of five siblings. His father, Charles B. Kelly Sr., was born in Virginia and moved to Philadelphia, where he met his beautiful wife-to-be, Juliet Elzie, from Crisfield, MD. Charles was employed as a bus driver for the Pennsylvania Transportation Company. And

Juliet was employed by the City of Philadelphia as a data processing analyst. In the early 1950s, they resided at 1519 West Edgeley Street, Philadelphia (North Philly), approximately five city blocks from the well-known Uptown Theater.

The neighborhood consisted of thirty row homes per city block. Three storeys tall with white marble steps. Families on our block were very close, and we looked out for each other. If your parents were working and you misbehaved, the neighbors became your parents and they would physically or verbally correct you. And when your parents came home and received the news from the neighbor, you were corrected a second time. That's probably how I learned to dance— by shaking. I was scared to death. I resided on a well-organized block; we did things together.

My education and employment consisted of the following:

Graduate of John Bartram High School, Philadelphia, PA, two years of college at Temple University (Sociology) and one year of college at the University of Delaware (Law Enforcement). Employment history: operating room technician, respiratory therapist, Philadelphia Police officer, Pennsylvania Justice Department (Investigator) and Department of Defense Criminal Investigator, not overlooking my tenure in the music industry, which began in the early 1950s, while residing in North Philadelphia. My music career followed me into the year 2005. During that time, I sang with such superstars as Eddie Holman, and Patsy Holt/Patti LaBelle. I organized and sang with The Volcanos, and got the group its first recording contract with Arctic Records. Several years later, when disco entered the music industry, the groups name was changed from The Volcanos to The Trammps. In the calendar year of 2003, I established my own record company, Prettyboy Records. In 2004, I began to manage and record jazz and gospel groups such as the Metropolitan Male Ensemble, and Northbound. My hobbies and interests are scuba diving, model trains, ham radio, fishing, and music.

Behind the Curtains

with

THE VOLCANOS
"Storm Warning"

and

The Grammy Award Winning

TRAMMPS
"Disco Inferno"

Chapter 1

When and Where did Stephen's Love for Music Begin?

In 1955, my love for music began to take root. As previously mentioned, I resided at 1519 W. Edgeley Street, in the heart of North Philadelphia. I was twelve years young. My neighbor, Mr. Eddie Neal, resided at 1517 W. Edgeley Street. Every Friday evening, I would see a clean cut group of fellas with processed hair enter Mr. Neal's home. Within minutes, Mr. Neal's house would become a musical jukebox. The singing and the harmony from those individuals rang out so clear and pretty, it would give you chills. The amazing thing about it all? They would sing without music.

One Saturday afternoon, I saw Mr. Neal exit his house to enter his car. He drove a 1950 Nash—it had four doors with a sloped back; it was maroon, and as big as an army tank. Mr. Neal would let my father borrow his car sometimes to drive our family down to Crisfield, MD, my mother's hometown. My three brothers, Charles, Michael, and Irvin, and my sister, Patsy and I, would spend the entire summer in Crisfield. We always had a great time there. With great curiosity I asked Mr. Neal who the fellas were that sang at his house on Friday evenings. With great pride and a smile he stated, "Those guys are going to be stars one day, Stevie. I manage them, and they call themselves "The Blue Notes"."

Of course, at that time I had never heard of "The Blue Notes", and I don't believe anyone else had heard of them either. The Man with the Goods, Georgie Woods of WDAS Radio, never played any songs by "The Blue Notes", nor did any other radio stations. What I didn't know is, Mr. Neal was rehearsing the group for their first recording. Approximately one month after my conversation with Mr. Neal, "The Blue Notes" released their first recording. It was entitled, "My Hero"—a silky love ballad. What a monster of a song. It gave the guys chills when they heard it, and it made the girls cry. After witnessing this great event, which began next door to me, no words can express how excited I became. Sometimes I would run to my mother and tell her of my dream to be a rock 'n' roll star. She would shake her head in a positive manner and smile. Did she approve, or did she see me as a child talking loudly and saying nothing? My mother was very talented; she could read music, and would put a record on the record player, listen to it, and play it on the piano.

One evening, I was sitting on the white marble steps in front of my house, chatting with another fellow who had the same dream as I, my schoolmate, Wyman Greir. Wyman was a peculiar individual. He was part of a large family that resided on the 1500 block of West Diamond Street. Diamond Street was the next block over from Edgeley Street. When Wyman went home, for whatever reason, he would always enter his house from the rear alley. I never saw him enter his house by way of the front door. The alley would be full of trash, and sometimes drunks. His dress attire wasn't the neatest either: sometimes Wyman would wear the same clothes for four days or more, and at times he literally stunk. Wyman also had a well-known enemy who carried a reputation as a bad guy, and the neighborhood bully. His name was Walter Robinson. When these two guys met up, it was like a cat and dog meeting. After being in each other's presence for a short period of time, one of them would say something insulting to the other, and it was on. The sad part about it all, there was never a winner or loser. As friends we couldn't stand by and watch them batter each other, so we would stop them from fighting. After each of them called each other a few choice names, they would each go their separate ways. Wyman and I attended Gillespie Jr. High School located at 18th and Pike Street in Philadelphia. We were both "A" students and close friends.

Wyman wasn't the only one who had it rough. As I was exceling in this world, my parents didn't have a lot of money. We weren't poor, nor were we wealthy. I guess you could say we were of the middle class. However, my parents had to raise five hungry children. On many occasions, I would have to wear shoes with holes in the bottom of them. My father would place a piece of cardboard inside the shoe to keep my feet off the ground. When the cardboard wore out, Dad would replace it with another piece. This went on until money was available to buy me or my siblings another pair of shoes. I remember wearing the same pair of wool pants to school every day. I never will forget them; they were dark brown with black stripes. I would wear them the entire week, and on Fridays, I would put them in the cleaners, get them out on Saturday, and put them back on when Monday came around. My classmates used to tease me to death. My parents' pay checks were always being squeezed, so asking my parents for money to see a show at the Uptown Theater was out of the question. Mom and Dad were strong believers in having the kids do chores around the house. My father showed us how to build shoe-shine boxes, and on Friday and Saturday nights, we would go to the corner of 15th and Susquehanna Avenue, in front of a bar called the Bright Spot and shine shoes. Sometimes our hard-earned money would be taken from us by bullies of the neighborhood. In order for me to receive income to see the rock 'n' roll shows at the Uptown Theater, I had to earn it.

One evening, my neighbor, Mr. Neal, pulled up in front of his house in his big car. He walked over to Wyman and me, and handed us a copy of "The Blue Notes" new release, "My Hero," and said, "Here you are Stevie, two copies of the group's record for you and your friend." He had just returned from doing a promotional tour on the road with "The Blue Notes". He could never get himself to call me Stephen; it was always Stevie. Heck, I didn't care—I was glad he talked to me. At that time, I disclosed to Mr. Neal that Wyman and I were talking about forming a singing group. I asked if he could manage us and give us some pointers in the business. With a smile he replied, "I'll be glad to Stevie." In 1956, Wyman and I formed our first singing group. It consisted of five local members. We called ourselves "The Superbs", and on Saturday nights, if Mr. Neal was in town, we would be at his house learning to sing harmony and do dance routines. We had to rehearse on Saturdays, because during the week we had to keep up with our school work. And on Sundays, with our parents, we honored the Lord our God by attending church.

We became very good, and made and released our first recording under the management of Mr. Neal. Our first recording was entitled "Rainbow of Love"—but it wasn't a monster hit like "The Blue Notes" record. It didn't get much air play, but it felt good to know we had entered the world of entertainment. The most popular DJ at that time was Georgie Woods of WDAS radio. Georgie began giving rock 'n' roll shows at the Uptown Theater, located on Broad Street in the vicinity of Dauphine Street. Another WDAS radio personality who gave rock 'n' roll shows was Lord Fauntleroy, better known in real life as John Bandy. Their Uptown productions consisted of well-known artists such as "Little Anthony and The Imperials", "James Brown and The Flames", "The Dells", "Shep and The Limelights", "The Platters" … You name them, they were there.

Georgie Woods

To see a show at the Uptown Theater, kids under fifteen could get in for fifty cents if they entered the theater before noon. After noon, it would cost seventy-five cents. The cost for adults for the first show, before noon, was a dollar and twenty-five cents. In the afternoon, it would cost a dollar seventy-five. To earn this type of money, I had to shine shoes, carry groceries for people who shopped at the A&P Super Market, located in the same block as the Uptown Theater, and complete my obligations when it came to household chores—scrubbing our white marble steps, and cleaning my bedroom. My father was very strict, but he was also a hustler. He taught us the meaning of a dollar.

John Bandy "Lord Fauntleroy"

I'll never forget this: one Christmas Eve, he was selling Christmas trees on the corner of 16th and Edgeley Street. When a lady came up to purchase a tree, he grabbed one out of the bunch to show her. He told her he was running a special on the tree he was holding in his hands. He banged it on the ground to get the branches to fall down, told the lady it was a full tree, and it should serve her well. When the lady asked him to turn the tree around, he turned around with the tree and replied, "See lady? It's a full tree." Believe it or not, my dad sold the tree to the lady. When Christmas came around and I was in the company of my dad, I would always remind him of that fantastic sale; it would bring a smile to his face. A dollar bill had great value in 1950. Heck, you could purchase a loaf of bread for ten cents.

For the life of me, I could never understand why a person hanging out in a dirty smelly bar with the stench of smoke and liquor would come outside, get a shoe shine, and re-enter the bar. The lights in the bar were too low for anyone to see the shine.

Everything didn't always run smoothly. Yep! There were neighborhood thugs. One person in particular comes to mind. He called himself "Worm," and he sure looked the part. He was cross-eyed and always carried a tree branch in the place of a crane. When he saw you, your day was over. He would walk up to you, poke your pants pockets with his tree branch and if he heard the sound of coins in your pockets, he would order you to empty them. On several occasions, he took the money I had earned for the Uptown Theater. What a tearful event that was ...

Photo of the Uptown Theater and Georgie

Out of disgust, I grew smarter. As I earned my money for the Uptown Theater, I would convert my change into dollar bills and hide the money in my socks. If Worm showed up, he would only get small change. The early bird gets the Worm.

Stephen C. Kelly

Chapter 2

My First Rock 'n' Roll Show at the Uptown Theater

Well it finally happened; I saw a rock 'n' roll show at the Uptown Theater. What an experience! I saw Georgie Woods in person with his cow bell. It was a great show. Appearing were "The Blue Notes", "The Moonglows", "The Dream Lovers", "Moms Mabley", "The Schoolboys", Frankie Lymon and "The Teenagers" and others. The house band was the Doc Bagby Orchestra. Even though I was a patron in the audience, it was such a thrill to be inside the Uptown Theater. They would have approximately three shows per day. In between the shows, they would show the Three Stooges and Flash Gordon. Man, did I get tired of watching the Three Stooges. I couldn't leave unless I saw two shows. Remembering how I felt when I recorded my first record with Mr. Neal, I jumped right back in the swing of things. I would gather some of the guys from the neighborhood and we would sing doo-wop songs for hours. We sang songs by by "The Clifftones", "Oh Little Girl of Mine", Frankie Lymon and "The Teenagers", "I'm Not A Juvenile Delinquent", "The Dream Lovers", "When We Get Married", "Little Anthony and The Imperials", "Traveling Stranger", you name it, we sang it.

At 16th and Edgeley Street, on 16th Street, another Kelly family resided. There were two Kelly families. Believe it or not, between the two families there were three people with the name of Charles. There were two in my family, and one in the family that resided on 16th Street. The Charles Kelly who resided on 16th Street was much younger than my oldest brother and father. But man, could he sing. He sang lead to most of our doo-wop songs. We would sing on the corners under street lights until the red police cars came to chase us off the corner. Believe me, in those days, if a police officer told you to leave the corner, you left without the intention of returning. During my tenure on Edgeley Street, I met a lot of people in the neighborhood. Some people I saw frequently, but I never took the opportunity to introduce myself. The next two individuals that I will be introducing to you fall into that category. Stanley Wade and his brother Harold Wade would frequent Edgeley Street with their mother to visit relatives. They were always well-dressed in suits and ties, and always stood in the doorway of their relatives' home. They watched us play stick ball, but never spoke a word. As faith would have it, in 1957, my family moved to West Philly, and at that time I was attending Gillespie Junior High School at 18th and Pike Street. When my mother transferred me to Sayre Junior High at 58th and Walnut Street, guess who was seated in my English class—Harold Wade. We will address Stanley and Harold later in this biography. The transition from North Philly to West Philly was not an easy transition; I lost all of my North Philly friends.

In 1957, I graduated from Sayre Junior High School at 58th and Walnut Street, and entered John Bartram High School at 67th and Elmwood Avenue, Philadelphia. That's when my ambition to re-enter the music industry returned. Music was everywhere in John Bartram High School: music classes, talent shows, and students who wanted to become musicians and singers. When some of the wannabe singers gathered inside the boys' restroom to lay down a song or two during our lunch period, you could hear the smooth echoes of their doo-wop harmony bouncing off the walls of the restroom.

One of the students who participated in the doo-wop singing was a fellow named Sylvester Rose. Man, did he have a beautiful controlled falsetto voice. He could have carried the nickname of "Bird" without a doubt. In Bartram, we had what was called a study period. During that time, you were allowed to catch up on any assignments you might have missed, or study for an upcoming test. All grade levels would be present. During one of those study periods, I bumped into the golden voice himself, Sylvester Rose. After introducing myself, I asked Sylvester if he would be interested in starting a singing group, with him as the lead singer. He gave a short burst of laughter and replied, "Why not." Jointly, we began a search for additional members.

Talking about looking a gift horse in the mouth: I was seated in my English class when I glanced over to the last row of seats in the classroom, and noticed a familiar face. I couldn't remember where I had seen the individual before, but I knew him from somewhere. After class, I approached him and he said his name was Harold Wade, at which time we exchanged our thoughts and connections. We traced our connection back to the 1500 block of West Edgeley Street (North Philly) as being our common grounds. What was so ironic was, Harold was currently living at 830 South 56th Street in Southwest Philly, and I was living at 5550 Delancey Street, also in Southwest Philly. As a matter of fact, just seven blocks away from each other.

I shared my dream of starting a singing group and told him about Sylvester Rose. Harold chuckled and replied that Stanley (his brother), John Hart Jr. (his cousin), along with a guy named Kenny Gamble, were background singers for Herb Johnson. Herb had a record out called "Have You Heard." Harold, who was known by the nickname "Doc," said he wanted to try something new because things were slow when it came to booking weekend gigs with Herb. Doc spoke to Stanley, who was in agreement with Doc to start a group. This was the beginning of a beautiful relationship. Even though we were all attending the same school, it took some time to bring everybody together. It was like pulling teeth for me. Some members were talking loudly and doing nothing. When we finally got together, the group members were Harold and Stanley Wade, Sylvester Rose and me. Harold sang baritone, Stanley sang first tenor, I sang second tenor, and Sylvester sang lead. After a few months of rehearsals, things came together, and the word was out: "There's a bad group in Bartram." Even the music teachers got involved with the music scene. They began arranging talent shows for the students. John Bartram High was all of that! We had so much talent in the school, we could have put on a concert.

Sylvester lost interest in the group and left. We were just singing in and around school and he wanted to do more. What more could we do? We had to finish our education. But as the old saying goes, "when one door closes another one opens." Guess who became our lead singer? I'll give you a small clue. Her name was Patricia Holt.

Give up? Well, it's time to let the cat out of the bag. Patricia Holt later became Patti LaBelle. Remember "The Bluebells" in 1962? They had the hit record "I Sold My Heart to the Junkman."

Before this blessing occurred for Patti, she was a member of her church choir and resided in a little community called Elmwood, PA. She later relocated to 58th and Washington Avenue, Southwest Philly. With Patsy as our lead singer, we blew everyone else that participated in the talent shows away. Oh yeah! We even blew Eddie Holman away; he attended Bartram. However, he wasn't a superstar at that time. Eddie liked what he heard, and his interest fell on the background voices of the group. As a matter of fact, Eddie invited Doc, Stanley, and me to his house to hear a song he had written. He wanted us to put the background voices to it. Well, the song just didn't make much sense. He called it "Pop-Eye Vi." It was an up-tempo song and he could play it on his piano. Oh well, we gave it our best shot.

As for the three musketeers, Doc, Stanley, and Steve, our mission wasn't complete. We needed a bass singer, so we picked up another Bartram knight. His name was Robert Jones. Rob resided in the 5900 block of Spruce Street—yep, he was another Southwest Philly member. This made it convenient for us to rehearse. It sort of reminds you of the Motown artists; most of them were from the same neighborhoods. With Patsy on board, the name "Patti and the Epsilons" was born.

Before I forget, allow me to mention this one fella. If there was ever a nerd, this guy was it. His name was Tracy Harris. Tracy wore thick glasses and did not look the part of a recording artist. He was a nice guy, but he could not sing or hold a note, even if his life depended on it. If I was of age and could drink, his singing would have driven me to drink. He always called me "Kelly," never "Stephen." He was a Bartram knight as well. When the talent shows and music started popping at school, he wanted to get in on the scene. One day, he asked me to attend one of his rehearsals, just to give his group some pointers. I agreed. Man, was that a big mistake. He had four guys singing background, and he was trying to sing the lead. Those entangled voices sounded like a 78-speed record being played in 33-speed mode. The notes were sliding all over the place. Sorry Trace, no pun intended.

After graduating from Bartram, the group members kept in touch with each other, and continued to rehearse. The background singers had to drink beer and suck on lemons to keep our voices tuned to Patsy's high voice. It also helped the harmony to become clear and tight. However, not having a crystal ball to foresee the future, the guys in the group didn't know what Patsy's mother, Chubby, had planned for her daughter. Our wonderful relationship with Patsy, as her friends and background singers, was coming to an end. Chubby cut a deal for Patsy with Harold B. Robinson, the owner of a car dealership located at the end of North Broad Street in Philly. In the basement of the dealership was a recording studio, and a music producer by the name of Bobby Martin. Mr. Martin was to be the future songwriter and arranger for Patsy. Talking about hard times knocking at your front door, this was it. The move was great for Patsy, and we were glad for her, but it left us out in the cold. Patsy went with her mother's choice and honored her decision. Patsy was introduced to three beautiful ladies from Camden, New Jersey: Sarah Dash, Cindy Birdsong, and Nona Hendryx, who later became "The Bluebells".

Bobby Martin

"The Bluebells"

I will always honor Patsy, and never forget her late mother
chubby and her late sisters Barbra and Jackie.

Chapter 3

Out of the Military and Back into the Music World

With so many negative interruptions within the music industry and the possibility of being drafted, Harold and I joined the U.S. Naval Reserves Buddy-Buddy plan. Believe you me, it was anything but a Buddy-Buddy plan. We never sailed on the same ships together for our training duty. The only time we were together was when we attended classes in building 662 on the Philadelphia Naval Base. And that was once a month on Wednesday nights. I never stopped singing. On one of my training ships out of New York City, the U.S.S. Kidd, were shipmates who loved to sing. After all, it was New York, New York. If we didn't have the duty watch, we would get together on the fantail of the ship and sing doo-wop. In 1963, Harold and I were honorably discharged from the Navy. Again I pursued my dream of becoming a recording artist.

Reorganizing the group members wasn't hard because we resided in the same neighborhood—Southwest Philly. But I didn't have a lead singer. Doc, Rob, and I canvassed the neighborhoods of Southwest Philly for a lead vocalist. As God would have it, we located another female vocalist, right in our own back yard. Her name was Teresa Chambers. Teresa resided at 57th and Larchwood Avenue in Philly. She was petite, had a nice smile, dressed well, and was single. She wasn't a Bartram knight; she attended West Philly High School. One for West Philly High school. Teresa showed great interest in the group. We rehearsed at least twice a week. Our harmony became so tight, it had a ring to it. We called ourselves "Terry and The Epsilons", and the name was getting around Philly. Finally, it was our time to step into the arena and compete with other groups. The proprietor of the Tally Paradise Club, located at 16th and Fitzwater Street in South Philly, asked us to participate in a talent show he was having at the club. The host would be a well-known recording artist by the name of Solomon Burke. Solomon was with Atlantic Records, and later changed over to MGM Records.

He recorded such song as "Cry to Me," "If You Need Me," "Everybody Needs Somebody to Love," and many more. His tenure covered the 1960s. We knew he would draw a large crowd because of who he was. That evening, we went up against five Philly groups and ended up taking home the winning trophy: cash!

Let me make something perfectly clear. We weren't the only group in the neighborhood. There was a vocal group called "The V-Tones", located in the vicinity of 46th and Spruce Street. They heard about us and offered the group a challenge. Now we were involved in the battle of the groups. We accepted their challenge, and we were to meet in the basement of one of their members' homes on 46th Street. As we walked the ten blocks, 56th Street to 46th Street, we tuned up our voices by singing songs. I will never forget the looks on some of the pedestrians' faces as we approached or passed them. They were admiring our singing. Some of them stopped for a brief moment to listen to us. We were impressed, but didn't show it.

The V-Tones' style of singing was very different from ours. They sang ballads; the type of songs "The Platters" would sing, such as "My Prayer," "Smoke Gets in Your Eyes," etc. They were very good at what they sang. They even sang "Hava Nagila" and they tore it up. Most of their gigs were booked at Jewish events. Our songs were of the current R&B charts. Because there were two different styles of singing, we had no winners or losers. We exchanged business cards and addressed the possibility of doing engagements together. My group had a cat hanging on the fence, and we didn't know when he was going to jump off. I'm speaking of Rob Jones, our bass vocalist. Rob's ambition was to attend college. His first year was approaching fast. Well, somebody in "The Epsilons" was living right; the good Lord laid another blessing on us. As faith would have it, William Luby, "The V-Tones" bass singer, asked to join my group. Luby wanted to get away from singing ballad songs and he wanted to stretch out a little more into the R&B scene.

Well, the cat jumped off the fence and Luby entered the group. It was a perfect exchange. We continued rehearsing at my house, and the group's harmony became even tighter than before. But all of a sudden, the lights went out again. Our lead vocalist, Teresa, was having a problem concentrating on our songs during rehearsals. We had no idea what was going on, or what was behind it all. Finally at one of our rehearsals, it all came to the surface. Teresa's boyfriend, Lawrence Taylor, showed up at our rehearsal and told Teresa to stop singing and leave the rehearsal. Unbeknownst to us, Lawrence was very jealous, and he didn't want Teresa in our company. After weighing the pros and cons, we decided to ask Teresa to leave the group. Did Lawrence Taylor ever marry Teresa? No. Did Teresa miss the opportunity of a lifetime? At that time, one wouldn't have known, but the future proved the answer to be … yes.

Stephen C. Kelly

THE VOLCANOS
Harold Wade – Stephen Kelly – Stanley Wade
Eugene Jones

Well here we go again, searching for another lead vocalist. I had been down this road so many times, I asked the street commissioner to take down the street sign. I knew the road by heart. Forgive me, I just had to vent. Again the group was in the middle of a creek without a paddle. If we look at the chain of events, you will notice that when one door closes, another door opens up, with better goodies inside the second door. The pain we endure to get to the top. At any rate, thank God for William Luby. Luby knew a guy who loved to sing, and probably would love to join the group. He was known by the nickname "Cools," but his real name is Eugene Jones. From here on, we will address him in this biography as Gene. Luby brought Gene to one of our rehearsals, and we thought he had brought in James Brown. His looks, singing and movements were like those of James Brown. His hairstyle was out of sight; I don't know how he kept the hair in place on top of his head. You talk about hard labor; Gene knew what it meant. He was a family man. His employment consisted of plucking chickens and buffing cars. He wanted a break in life, and felt that break could come by way of the music industry. He loved singing. Receiving good vibes from Gene, the group got busy.

As the group was sharpening the saw, we paid attention to the different styles of recording artists and the songs they sang. Of course we loved James Brown, and we also focused on the styles of other groups, such as "Lee Andrews and The Hearts", "The Orlons", "The Dovells", "The Times", "Danny and The Juniors", and many more. We started listening to American Bandstand when Bob Horn hosted the show. Bandstand was located at 46th and Market Street, in Philly. Of course you know the story behind Bob Horn: he just couldn't leave those pretty little girls alone, and was asked to leave the show. When Dick Clark came on board, he took American Bandstand to another level. The dancers on the show would rate the records. If it had a good beat, the record received air play, and stayed on the show until it dropped off the charts. If I remember correctly, Jerry Blavat was one of the American Bandstand dancers. Today, he is recognized as one of the music industry's most knowledgeable historians when it comes to Twentieth Century Music, Rhythm and Blues, and doo-wop songs.

When Gene entered the group, we knew we had to come up with another name. We had become so dynamic, "The Epsilons" just didn't cut it. We wanted a fresh start and a new direction. We also visited the thought of being a self-contained group. However, we needed instruments. I worked at a gas station pumping gas. My rent at home was sixty dollars a month. My monthly income was about one hundred and twenty dollars. Out of that I had to buy clothing and take care of my personal needs. After all was said and done, there wasn't much money left. Doc and Stanley were employed at the Sun Ship Building Company, located in Chester, PA. Their responsibilities were great also. Luby was the only one with a well-paying job; he worked for the U.S. Postal Service. But he didn't need an instrument. Gene had a wife and two or three kids to support—you can't give up money when you're plucking chickens and buffing cars.

After saving my few pennies, I brought my first drum set from a pawn shop located at 10th and South Street in South Philly. The entire set cost one hundred and ten dollars, and it was gold sparkle in color. I was so proud of that set. Now keep in mind when it comes to a professional set of drums two high hat cymbals could cost three hundred dollars, and crash cymbals could cost three hundred and eighty dollars each. A ride cymbal could cost two hundred and fifty dollars each, not overlooking the cost for the hardware and the drums. The total cost for cymbals was nine hundred and thirty dollars. Can you imagine the value of my drum set? I paid only one hundred and ten dollars for everything. Believe you me, later it didn't prove to be such a good deal, but I didn't know any better—all I wanted to do was play drums. I thought I was hot stuff!

Now it was Harold's turn. Where were we going to get this guitar? Three members of the group, me being one of the three, went to Eighth Street Music Center in Philly, just to browse. We wanted to see what we were up against. When we entered the store, we noticed a black and white used Silvertone guitar hanging on the wall. We removed the guitar so Doc could examine it. It looked and felt good, and didn't appear to be damaged. We took the guitar over to the sales clerk, who was busy doing something other than selling the store's merchandise. When we asked how much the guitar was selling for, he looked at us with disgust and mumbled something. To this day I don't what he said, but it wasn't good. We were well-dressed and displayed proper mannerism. However, he never gave us a price. Needless to say, we acquired the guitar, but how we got it ... well, some things are best left to one's imagination.

A few weeks later, Stanley showed up at rehearsal with a used Fender bass guitar in a carrying case. Stanley had a little luck with his purchase; his mother helped him buy his guitar, which was a good thing. As for other instruments, Gene had an old hollow-box guitar he used when he was writing songs. It served the purpose. Now, we needed a permanent place for rehearsals. Prior, we were sharing rehearsal locations at different members' homes. Now that instruments were involved—drums, amps etc.—we needed a fixed location. So I cut a deal with my parents for the use of our basement. It went a little like this: No weekday rehearsals; You may rehearse on Friday or Saturday evenings only; Be in by 6:30 pm and out by 8:30 pm; All instruments and bodies will enter the basement through the back door, never the front door. Of course the back door part came from my father. As human beings, we couldn't enter the front door. My father raced homing pigeons, and those dirty birds always came through the front door. To add insult to injury, he used to enter the living room area via the front door, with the birds in a cage, carry them up the steps to the second floor, and enter a closet were he had built a trap door leading to the roof. That's where the loft for the birds was erected. This used to drive my mother insane; pigeon feathers would be all over her nice carpets.

As previously stated, my mother was employed by the City of Philadelphia. Some way, somehow, Kenny Gamble got the news I was involved with a singing group. Either Kenny or his brother worked for the city—that's where and how the connection was made with my mother. This was before Kenny became the legendary proprietor of Philadelphia International Records. At any rate, Kenny resided on the 5400 block of Osage Avenue, in Southwest Philly. Osage Ave was one block south of where I resided. On one occasion, I remember Kenny stopping by my house. He had this hot song bouncing around in his head, and he wanted me to listen to it. He sat down at my mother's piano and began to play. The melody and lyrics to the song were great. However, my focal point was to be a recording artist, not a writer. Oh, if I could turn back the hands of time.

A couple of months passed, and the group's progress was unbelievable. We could sing and play our songs at the same time. I will never forget, at one of our rehearsals, my mother was in the kitchen cooking, and all of a sudden she came running down the basement steps. We stopped singing, looked at her, and then looked at each other. Mom smiled and said, "I just wanted to see who was doing all of that screaming." She returned to the kitchen. It was Gene; he was feeling every song we were singing that night. We were ready to shop for a recording contract.

Acknowledging my mother, Juliet Kelly. My mother was a spiritual person. She sang and played piano for the church choir at Mt. Pleasant Baptist Church, which was located at 56th and Vine Street, Southwest Philly, as well as the Seventh Day Adventist Church, 48th and Market Street Philly, and the Seventh Day Adventist Church located in Salisbury, MD. The church enjoyed her dedication and playing so much, some churches provided an escort service for her in order to assure themselves she would arrive at their church to play. You could put a record on a record player, play it, and take it off, and just by listening for that short period of time, she cloud play the entire song. She played for church choirs of all faiths until she was eighty-two years old. At eighty-four cancer struck, and God called her home. She was a gifted person. She is dearly missed.

Mr Charles B. Kelly Sir and Stephen, enjoying a day of fishing in Crisfield, MD

Mrs. Juliet Kelly, Stephen's mother

Two wonderful parents who are truly missed, with love; Stephen

Chapter 4

Shopping for a Record Deal

In early 1964, after rehearsing so long and so hard, I decided to try to market the group. The first person we auditioned for was a fellow who alleged he was affiliated with major record companies in New York City. His name, at present, escapes me, but I know he resided in the vicinity of Broad and Only, on Only Avenue. The group went to his home and auditioned without our instruments. We sang our hearts out, and people were standing outside of his home listening to us. When we finished singing, he asked us if we had any original tunes. We did, but he never got to hear them. We had to be careful, so I told the group not to sing them. I think he wanted to steal them and later try to sell them to a record company. When all was said and done, the individual had nothing to offer us. He made off-the-wall comments like, "You boys are singing that Deacon Brown stuff." Surely, we weren't singing spirituals, so his comment was very inappropriate. One thing for sure was, we had no problem finding his front door. When we exited his home, the people outside started clapping. That told us we were on the right track, but at the wrong station.

My next marketing plan was to make an appointment to meet with a radio personality like Georgie Woods or Jimmy Bishop of WDAS Radio. I didn't want to meet with Kay Williams; he was also a radio jock at WDAS. There was nothing but bad news floating around about him. He managed "Ruby and The Romantics". I was granted an appointment with Jimmy Bishop after speaking to Otto Kershaw, Chief of Security for WDAS, approximately seven times. I was determined to meet with Jimmy Bishop. I was granted an appointment with Jimmy while he was on the air. As I entered the broadcasting booth, I noticed Jimmy was in the company of Kenny Gamble. I divulged to Jimmy the group's history and what we had to offer, and requested an audition. It must have taken forty-five minutes to an hour before he agreed to listen to the group. I have reason to believe Kenny had some input in Jimmy Bishop making his decision. After all, Kenny was well aware of the group before I met Jimmy Bishop. Jimmy set my group up for an audition with Harthon Records, located at 5944 Chestnut Street, Philadelphia.

Harthon Records was owned by three musically inclined gentlemen. They were Weldon Arthur McDougal III, Johnny Stiles, and Luther Randolph. Before I continue with the biography of The Volcanos and The Trammps, allow me to give these three gentlemen acknowledgement. Let's place the spotlight on Weldon Arthur McDougal III. He attended West Philadelphia High School and was a native Philadelphian. Weldon was a born hustler; he knew how to earn an honest dollar. In his younger years, he delivered newspapers in his neighborhood, which would be the road for him to meet his friend and soon-to-be-partner, Johnny Stiles. In the mid 1950s, Weldon formed his first singing group, "The Larks". Their first recording was released in 1961: "It's Unbelievable," on Sheryl Records.

From the mid 1950s to the year 2010, Weldon A. McDougal contributed to the musical evolution of the sound of Philadelphia for over four decades. As a songwriter, recording artist, group bandleader, and independent producer, he has helped shape and influence the creation and development of the Philly sound since the mid 1950s. As a founding member and co-owner of the now-legendary Harthon/Dyno Dynamics record labels alongside Luther Randolph and Johnny Stiles, Weldon produced diverse local Philly artists such as "Eddie Holman", "The Volcanos", "Barbara Mason", "Larry Clinton", "Nella Dodds", "Cindy Gibson", "Herb Ward", and many others. Weldon was very instrumental in the production of Barbara Mason's hit record "Yes I'm Ready," which is one of the first examples of the sweet, lush, orchestrated sound that came to be called Philly Soul. In the 1970s Weldon continued to produce while working nationally for Motown Records.

THE LARKS

Johnny Stiles attended John Bartram High School and was also a native Philadelphian. During his tenure at Bartram High, he was a member of a doo-wop group called "The Medallions". John was a well-known violinist, and he could play every string instrument known to man. The Medallions' members consisted of Harrison Scott (saxophonist), Herman Carter (bass guitar), Lonnie Brown (drummer), Freddie Simmons (pianist), and Johnny Stiles (string instruments). In 1954, the group reinvented themselves when some members left, and new ones were added. They then called themselves "The Manhattans".

Weldon Arthur McDougal III

The group's members were Harrison Scott (sax), Darrell Smallwood (drums), Hollis Floyd (piano), and Johnny Stiles (guitar). Luther Randolph mastered his education via the school system of Media Pennsylvania, where he was born and raised. He started playing piano at the age of eight and became so well-versed, in music he began playing classical compositions for audiences. By the age of fourteen, he was part of a jazz quartet. He played with such musicians as Marcus Melleray (trumpet player for Ray Charles), Harthon Miles (played with Jerry Butler), and a drummer named Niles Hope. After returning home from the military,

Luther received a phone call from his main rival, Johnny Stiles. They located a drummer by the name of Norman Connors, formed a trio, and made their first recording on Harthon Records, called "Cross Roads."

Here we have three gentlemen who wanted to make a positive difference in their lives and the lives of their recording artists. You read their biographies, now let me introduce to you their functions and responsibilities: Weldon McDougal III, singer and producer for Harthon Records; Johnny Stiles, violinist and string arranger for Harthon Records; Luther Randolph, organist and chart arranger for Harthon Records.

Luther – Weldon - Johnny

Three good-hearted men who wanted to make a difference in the music industry. As we continue with the biography of The Volcanos and The Trammps, you will read how Jimmy Bishop penetrated the hearts and minds of these three innocent souls by manipulating them and stealing recording artists from their record company.

If you have ever seen or read the classic novel "A Christmas Carol" by Charles Dickens, you are about to be introduced to Jimmy Bishop, whose lifestyle resembles that of the character Scrooge in the novel.

Remember the scene where Scrooge wanted to take over all of the investors' shares? I'll leave it there for now.

JIMMY BISHOP

WDAS

My group got an opportunity to audition for Harthon Records. Present were Weldon McDougal III and Johnny Stiles. After hearing the group, they found us to be so dynamic that they called us The Volcanos. Make no mistake about it, the name Volcanos belonged to Harthon Records. Under the umbrella of Harthon Records were such artists as "The Twilights", "Jo-Ann Jackson and The Dreams", "Barbara Mason", "Eddie Holman", "Herb Ward", " The Volcanos", and many more.

How does the saying go? "When it rains it pours." As we continued rehearsing with Harthon Records, a roadblock came into my personal life. At home, my father was charging my brothers and me sixty dollars each per month for rent. Allow me to introduce my siblings to you: my youngest brother Irvin, next in line is yours truly, then Michael, then my late brother Charles, and my late sister Patricia. All of us had to pay our dues at home if we wanted a roof over our heads. The head of the household was Mr. Charles B. Kelly Sr.—my dad.

Well, in order for me to keep the group afloat, I had to find another job that paid more money. We weren't gigging and we still had expenses. I applied for employment with the City of Philadelphia by taking a city exam. I became an operating room trainee at Philadelphia General Hospital. When my father found out, he said, "Congratulations, son, on your new job." I thought I was getting ahead of the game. Well, as life would have it, my rent went from sixty dollars to one hundred dollars a month. That was the last straw.

When I approached my father about the rent increase, we got into it hot and heavy. You see, he never brought us the bad news—he would always have my mother break the bad news to us, no matter what the bad news was. He wanted to make her look like the villain, but we knew better. My mother was my mom, my friend, my heart, and my support system. All she ever gave us was love, advice, and support. Don't get me wrong, if you got out of line, you would hear about it. Sometimes she would spare the rod, but when you deserved it, you got it.

It's funny now, but it wasn't funny then. I remember the times the family would spend the summer in my mother's hometown, Crisfield, MD. When you did something wrong, her mother would tell you to go out in the field and bring in the thickest switch off a tree that you could find. If it wasn't thick enough, she would send you back for another one. When she got finished with you, that switch would be a pile of twigs.

After the heated argument with my father, which was to no avail, I could not get him to understand what I was trying to accomplish with my group. He was

---

Behind the Curtains   **25**

only interested in green dollar bills. That night, which I will never forget, I got so upset I lost control of my thoughts entirely; I didn't know I could get so angry. I ran upstairs to the second-floor back bedroom, opened the window, and threw my clothing and personal belongings out the window.

I spent the night sitting on the street curb of the 5500 block of Delancey Street, with my belongings in large plastic bags. The incident devastated my mother so, it made her ill. Mom knew I didn't have a place to stay. But dear old Dad, he didn't care. That was the night I left home and never returned, except to visit my mother. If my father was at home, I would postpone my visit; I did not desire to be in his company.

After seeing how upset my mother was, I placed a phone call to my cousin Brian Nickens. Brian worked for Samuel's Optical Company located at 21st and Chestnut Street, Philadelphia. I informed Brian of what had taken place, and asked him to assist me with his vehicle. Brian was appalled at my father's actions, and he was willing to accommodate me to the fullest. When Brian arrived, we loaded my personal belongings in his little blue station wagon, and I asked him to drive me to the group's rehearsal. Brian drove me to 5944 Chestnut Street, the office where the group rehearsed. He stayed there with me until the completion of the rehearsal. Brian was very concerned, knowing I had no place to stay after rehearsal. You know, there's a quote—"God takes care of His own." That night He sure took care of me!

At our rehearsals there was this person who always seemed to manipulate his way into our rehearsals. His name was Bernie Broomer. Bernie resided at an apartment complex located at 63rd and Chestnut Street, Philadelphia. There was also another person who was always at the office when we came to rehearse. His name was Earl Young. Later, we found out Earl was a homeless person living at the office. He was the drummer for Harthon Record Company. And of course, Harthon Records owned the building at which we rehearsed.

The night I became homeless, my participation with the group was lacking. I could not focus on my note—I kept sliding off it. I was worried about my mother and the thought of me being homeless struck. What an empty and scary feeling you get. As long as I was with the group members, it didn't seem to be so bad. But when we took a break, I felt this deep sadness and an unsettled feeling in my lower stomach. I became unnerved; I was scared. Brian told Weldon what had occurred, Weldon spoke to Bernie, and Bernie took me in as a roomer. After rooming with Bernie for approximately three months, I got to know him a little better. Bernie showed great interest in the group so I decided to make him the group's road manager. After saving money for my first apartment, I later moved into Chatem Court apartments, 49th and Locust, Philadelphia. Man! I was so happy! I could think clearer, I had freedom, and I could do as I darn well pleased.

After I got settled in my new apartment, I reached out for Earl Young, knowing how it felt to be homeless for just one night. I felt obligated to help him. I introduced myself to the manager of the complex, Earl Lego, and asked if they were hiring. Mr. Lego had a janitorial position open; it required some sweeping and snow shoveling around the complex. Also, the janitor would have to set trash out on trash day. The position came with a free one-bedroom apartment. I couldn't wait to tell Earl. Needless to say, he got the job. Every time you saw Earl, he had a pair of drum sticks in his hands. If you didn't know him you would think he was Chinese and they were a pair of chop sticks. Seeing how dedicated he was about playing drums, I gave him the opportunity to play drums for the group. Earl was a good drummer and he was exceling with his talent. However, some people forget where they came from and who helped them get there. This statement will mirror itself as we get further into the biography.

In 1964, The Volcanos were introduced to their first recording session at Virtue Recording Studios, located at Broad and Columbia Avenue, Philadelphia. The proprietor of the studio was Frank Virtue. Frank had a band called the Virtues. At nine years old, Frank was playing violin and switched over to the guitar in his later years. He was also a band leader for the U.S. Navy, located in Bainbridge, MD. His music career allowed him to be featured in shows with such great recording artists as the Nat King Cole Trio, the Stan Kenton Orchestra, Xavier Cugot, and Lionel Hampton. Frank had a peculiar way about him when he was around people in his recording studio. If you were seated in the control room, Frank would walk past you, and either stick his big butt in your face or step on your feet—and never excused himself. He weighed approximately 260 pounds.

You could never touch any of the equipment. He had a secret room in the back of the studio; nobody—and I do mean nobody—could enter that room except him or his wife Mary. It was said that was where he kept the mob's money. If you saw how Frank lived, you would think he was Elvis. Frank had a pink house shaped like a guitar, an airplane, expensive model trains from Germany, a recording studio ... you name it, he had it. To check on his pink house, he would fly over it in his plane. At his Philadelphia residence in the Great Northeast, yep, you guess it: he had a nice split-level home with a large swimming pool in his yard. Was Frank one of the bad guys? I don't think so, he always treated me well. I had the last Christmas dinner with him at his home before his passing. Is he a person who is missed? You bet he is.

The Volcanos' first recording was called "Baby," written by our lead singer Eugene Jones. The tune was a silky smooth blues ballad. The flip side of record was called "Storm Warning."

I will never forget how long we were in the recording studio—from evening to the wee hours of the morning. I'm talking approximately twelve hours or more per recording session. This was all new to us. We kept a little stash of wine on the side; it helped us get through it all. As for the record label we were going to sign with, we were never told which label we would be signing with or recording on. At that time, the record labels and production companies were not disclosed to us. We had no knowledge of the business; all we wanted to do was sing. Not overlooking the fact that our parents did not get involved with our music careers. Would it have been any different if they did? Yes, I truly believe it would have. We would have received better guidance, and all legal matters would have been properly addressed.

In 1964, Harthon Record Company had established their credentials as one of the premier production companies in the city of Philadelphia. Based on their track record and upcoming success, Frank Virtue recognized Harthon's success and gave them studio time on credit. Weldon, Johnny, and Luther were plugged in; it was time to start laying tracks. Air play for Harthon Records wasn't a problem. However, problems started to occur when the Harthon team became involved with Jimmy Bishop. Jimmy was like vapor gas: sneaky and deadly. Another key player was Harold Lipsius.

Stephen Kelly and Frank Virtue

Harold Lipsius was a lawyer by profession. He acquired part-ownership of a record pressing plant with record distribution when it was in default. In 1950, he started Jamie Record Company, and built it into one of the most powerful and influential record and distribution companies known to the music scene of Philadelphia. Jimmy Bishop was a well-known DJ on WDAS radio. How he got there will be addressed later in the biography.

As Harthon Records started building a reputation for producing quality records, Bishop noticed the radio audience was requesting to hear certain recording artists that were produced by Harthon. Harthon recording artists were flooding the charts. With such success happening for Harthon Records, Jimmy wanted in on the action. He approached the Harthon team and offered them the following deal:

Harthon Records would still be produced by Weldon, Johnny, and Luther. Harold Lipsius would press and distribute the product. And Jimmy would use his position to see that the records received air play. With everyone in agreement, a new production company was initiated.

The new production company consisted of five members who would receive equal shares of the company. The name of the new company, which was created by Jimmy Bishop, would be called Dyno Dynamics Productions, and the name of the record label would be Arctic Records. Personally, I think the name Dyno Dynamics needs a little help, and a label entitled Arctic is cold within itself. Was this Harthon's first warning? Harold and Jimmy weren't friends, nor were they each other's enemy. They got together because they needed each other. They were a team, and the team knew how to make money.

Chapter 5

The Rats Begin to Emerge

Another influential DJ was the legendary Georgie Woods. He was born on May 11, 1927, in Georgia. The Man with the Goods started his broadcasting career at age twenty-five on station WWRL (1600 AM), located in New York City. He was on the air for one hour. He retained that position for approximately three months. On January 7, 1953, he went to WHAT radio in Philadelphia. That's when the City of Brotherly Love became his new broadcasting home.

In 1956, Georgie relocated to WDAS radio in Philadelphia, where he became a true legend. Georgie used to have such sayings as "So nice, I gotta play it twice" and "Rock 'n' roll, everybody." Georgie loved to ring his cow bell and yell, "Rock 'n' roll!" He was the best at what he did and was a caring soul. If he could help you, he would. He became known as the Man with the Goods. No one could say that Georgie Woods was color-blind. He helped recording artists like "The Righteous Brothers"; he nicknamed them "The Blue-Eyed Soul Brothers." He played the heck out of "The Osmond Brothers" record "One Bad Apple" and played "The Magnificent Men" records as well.

Georgie Woods

In 1964, Georgie and WDAS management had a dispute. Georgie left WDAS and returned to WHAT. He was welcomed back with open arms by the owners of the station, Billy and Dolly Banks. It is alleged Jimmy Bishop had his hands in the mix. Bishop was full of greed and control, but we will return to Bishop after the honoring of the Man with the Goods, Georgie Woods. Georgie became a political activist. During early 1960s, Georgie was very instrumental in leading twenty-one buses of area residents to march with Dr. Martin Luther King in Alabama and Washington, DC. Georgie would later return to WDAS radio.

However, during his broadcasting transition, he was involved in broadcasting on WPGR radio, which was owned by broadcast pioneer Jerry Blavat.

He hosted his own dance party TV show on Channel 17, WPHL-TV, in 1966. A couple of years later Georgie moved the show to WIBF, Channel 29. He ran for political office in the city of Philadelphia. He hosted so-called freedom shows at the Uptown and Nixon Theaters to raise money for civil rights activities. He prevented rioting in the streets of Philadelphia. He was very instrumental in removing guns from the streets of Philadelphia in 1969. In 1988, he launched his own food product, Georgie Woods Potato Chips, which would sell over three million bags per year. He was very active in the March of Dimes crusade. And on November 18, 2005, Georgie Woods, broadcast pioneer, was inducted into the Hall of Fame. On June 18, 2005, Georgie Woods passed away. He is buried in the Delaware Valley area. Georgie's favorite song was an old spiritual song called "Oh Mary, Don't You Weep." If you must weep, weep for Georgie, for he was without a doubt humane.

As I previously stated, Jimmy Bishop was hungry for power; he was full of greed. He got his foothold at WDAS radio when he came to Philly and met the well-known radio personality, Louise Williams. If you love soapbox operas, you'll surely love "Welcome to Philly," featuring Jimmy Bishop, which will be coming up soon. As the new production company's staff continued to work with their artists, a bitter dispute ensued between members of the prior Harthon trio, Weldon, Johnny, and Luther, and the new Dyno Dynamics production company. Rates began to come out of the sewers. Jimmy Bishop started back stabbing Weldon, Johnny, and Luther. Bishop would hold private meetings with artists who were not signed, and force them into a binding recording contract, but as part of Harthon's record company. It is alleged he would tell them that if they signed with him, he could promise them air play and success. The artists didn't know Bishop was acting independently.

They looked at Bishop as being the person in charge, the person running the show. When artists started asking Weldon questions about their recording contracts, Weldon, Johnny, and Luther conducted a few meetings of their own with their artists. As a dog would have its bone, Jimmy was stealing the artists and their contracts from Harthon Record Company. The Harthon trio didn't approach Bishop's—his dealings were kept a secret and he was closely watched by Weldon. The sad part about this is the artists never knew where they stood or whom they could trust. As for my group, The Volcanos, we ended up on the Arctic record label. This was a segment of Jamie/Guyden Records.

Our first recording was called "Baby." It didn't make much noise when it got air play, so Jimmy Bishop started playing the other side. The other side was called "Storm Warning," written by Mr. Carl Fisher, lead singer for "The Vibrations". The song took off; it sold over sixty-five thousand copies in the Philadelphia area along. Nationally, we don't know how many records were sold—we were never told. In November 1965, Georgie Woods put on one of the largest rock 'n' roll shows ever held at the Uptown Theater. Appearing on the show were such recording artist as "Smokey Robinson and The Miracles", "The Four Tops", "Kim Weston", "The Volcanos", "The Royaletts", "The Show Stoppers", and many others. We did three shows on a weekday, and five shows on Thanksgiving Day and the weekends.

Now one thing must be perfectly understood: Jimmy Bishop was our manager. We were to be at the Uptown Theater, as Georgie would say, "for ten big exciting days." We loved Georgie Woods; he always treated us as friends and as professional artists. One of the things I think Georgie liked about The Volcanos was we were a drug-free singing group. No one in The Volcanos ever indulged in any type of narcotics, or smoked pot. And as of this writing, I can honestly say that still holds true today. Each member is still present on God's earth, except the late John Hart Jr. Before the passing of John Hart, he became a member of The Trammps in the early 1970s. We will address The Trammps in the second segment of the biography.

THE VOLCANOS

When we appeared on our first rock 'n' roll show in 1965, we owned one uniform each. It consisted of a blue sweater with a white dickey, blue pants and matching white shoes. Sort of like what "Frankie Lymon and The Teenagers" would wear. Jimmy Bishop never brought us a single outfit to wear on stage, on TV or anyplace else. We changed his name from Jimmy Bishop to Stingy Bishop. The recording artists from Motown were dressed to kill. Every artist on that show had several changes of clothing, except The Volcanos. Something had to be done, and we did it.

After rehearsal, we went to see our old friend Benny Krass at Krass Brothers clothing store in the 900 block of South Street in Philadelphia. You remember his saying, "If you didn't buy your suit from Krass Brothers, you were robbed"? Needless to say, Benny put us together. We ended up being one of the best-dressed acts on the show. We didn't make a lot of money from the show, because we had to pay Benny for our outfits. The ten-day show paid $700 for the entire group.

Of course the other artists made much more—we were the opening act. Artists from out of town were allowed to draw one third of their pay upfront. This was a normal practice; it allowed the artists to pay for their overnight accommodations. On that show, we had to ask for a draw so we could give Benny Krass a down payment on our outfits.

On that show, Georgie Woods introduced Jimmy Bishop to the Uptown Theater audience and allowed him to host the show. Bishop went over big with the audience; that's all he needed. Little did we know what the future would bring. We endured ten hard exciting days at the Uptown Theater. The lines outside the theater sometimes stretched more than three city blocks long. People wanted to see the rock 'n' roll show Georgie had put together. To this day, no other show at the Uptown Theater has ever mirrored it. It was a lot of hard work to perform show after show; at some points you felt like a prisoner. You couldn't leave the theater to get something to eat, not if you valued your life. Don't get me wrong—no one was looking to kill any of us, but if the groupie girls got their hands on you, they would rip you apart, just to get something they could cherish. I remember on Thanksgiving Day, we wanted to get some turkey. There was a lady who resided in the rear of the Uptown Theater; I believe her name was Mrs. Pearl. She cooked and sold dinners to the Uptown entertainers and the Uptown staff.

THE VOLCANOS

Well, after the first show, we decided we were going to get some turkey, no matter what. Otto was in charge of the back stage entrance door. On many occasions he forewarned us not to leave the theater once we entered. He also told us if we wanted something to eat, hire somebody to purchase the food for us. Well, we just wouldn't listen.

The group members wore long black leather coats. We put on our coats, buttoned them up to the very top—it was cold outside—and headed for the exit door. This is one time I should not have been the leader of the group. I told the guys to follow me, we are going to rush out the door and run across the street to Mrs. Pearl's house. Luck was not on our side. We told Otto to open the door, and we ran out. From out of nowhere, all these girls started screaming and grabbing us by whatever part of our clothing they could get their hands on. I was grabbed by the collar of my coat and nearly choked to death; my eyes were popping out of my head. To add insult to injury, a jealous boyfriend tried to punch the side of my head, and his punch landed on my right ear. At that, time the group went into defensive mode, and Otto came to our rescue. We never did that again.

Eating wasn't the only problem. The members of the group began to feel stiff and we encountered sore muscles from dancing on stage. In order to rejuvenate ourselves we had to drink wine. Thank God we brought the wine in at the beginning of the day. Bobby Rogers of The Miracles used to come to our dressing room. He wanted to know how we were staying so flexible during shows. He was feeling kind of sore himself. When we disclosed to him we had a foot locker full of Tokay wine, he fell over laughing. He couldn't handle the Tokay; he wanted some Wild Irish Rose wine. We didn't have any; however, the next day we sent our runner to get him a bottle. Yep! You read it right, a runner. After nearly getting killed we hired a runner. When entertainers do shows together, we live like family.

As I mentioned before, my group was the opening act for the show. Believe it or not, it was an important slot. We set the tempo for the entire show. When we got the audience fired up, the rest of the show would be a total blast! Every artist that followed behind you looked for the same response, or better. The only hard part about being first is, you were always the first act to get dressed. When the announcer said, "The half is in," it meant it was a half-hour before showtime. The announcement would come across speakers located in our dressing rooms, and it would also be written on a blackboard located back stage. After Smokey Robinson watched The Volcanos for three days, he approached Jimmy Bishop and asked him to sell the group to Motown. Smokey viewed us as being very dynamic with great stage presence. Jimmy declined Smokey's offer. It seemed as if Jimmy Bishop had some sort of resentment towards Motown. To this day, I will never understand his motives.

Smokey Robinson and The Miracles

Jimmy never did anything for The Volcanos and when a golden opportunity came from Motown, he shot it down. I truly believe Motown could have taken us in another direction and made us one of their top recording acts. After all, Motown had the writers and the musicians. The sad thing about it is, we will never know.

The Uptown Theater had a group of musicians who played an important part in providing the music for artists who appeared on the shows. Without them, the shows at the Uptown would not have been a success. We will get back to Stingy Bishop shortly—that's right, I said Stingy Bishop. It's not a typo. A fella named Bill Massey, a well-known trumpet player, was the Uptown Theater's first house band leader. But his leadership was short lived: he died of a drug overdose.

The second person in line was the great Harry Doc Bagly, who we will refer to as Doc in the biography. Doc's instrument was the Hammond organ. Man, he could make those pipes sing. He traveled with a trio doing large and small gigs. When Doc was asked to play for the Uptown Theater's band, he jumped right on it. Doc took over as the band leader for the house band. Doc and Georgie always started the rock 'n' roll shows with a composition called "Joy Ride Special." I can still hear the tune in my head. Doc quit the Uptown Theater after providing great music for many artists over a time span of ten years.

Douglas "Jocko" Henderson

After Doc's departure, another great team of band leaders and writers entered the picture. A gentleman named Sam Reed became the new house band leader. Also, another talented composer who played with Sam Reed's orchestra, was keyboardist, saxophonist, and arranger Leon Mitchell. Their positions required great concentration, charts had to be written, and special arrangements for the artists' music had to be implemented, as well as sheet music created for each and every band member. However, Sam Reed's tenure at the Uptown Theater was short lived. Guess who stole Sam Reed from the Uptown Theater. You guessed it: Jimmy Bishop.

Jimmy Bishop wasn't receiving the power and attention he thought he deserved, so he left the hosting position at the Uptown Theater. Before leaving, he put a bug in Sam Reed's ear and told him he could bring his band to the Nixon Theater, at 52nd and Market Street. And if he did so, he would be guaranteed a higher salary for his services.

Leon Mitchell

The Uptown Theater is located in North Philadelphia and the Nixon Theater was located in Southwest Philadelphia. The Uptown was known for its rock 'n' roll shows; the Nixon wasn't. Sam took Jimmy up on his offer.

But Sam Reed's ivory-playing buddy, Leon Mitchell, didn't take the bait. Leon stayed at the Uptown Theater with Georgie Woods and became the new house band leader for the Uptown Theater. Leon became so well-known by R&B jocks, he was all over the city of Philadelphia providing music charts, arrangements, and teaching music to students. Leon was even acknowledged by the late Douglas "Jocko" Henderson.

Every well-known black DJ located in Philadelphia wanted a piece of the pie Georgie Woods had. Jimmy Bishop tried the Nixon Theater, Jocko Henderson tried the State Theater, located at 52nd and Chestnut Street, one block South of the Nixon Theater. They all failed, except Georgie Woods, who continued to sit on his throne at the Uptown Theater, sometimes singing "Oh Mary, Don't You Weep"

Who is this smart fella who stood with Georgie? Allow me to introduce him to you. Leon Mitchell was born in August 1934, and reared in North Philadelphia. He attended public schools and was an honor graduate from Northeast High School in 1951. He was immersed in music ever since he turned pro as an alto saxophonist, immediately after graduation. Leon continued his music studies in the years that followed with Romeo Cascarino at Combs College, Jimmy Heath, and Bill Barron, the older brother of the fabulous jazz pianist Kenny Barron.

During Leon's ten years at the Uptown Theater, he associated himself with anybody who was into rhythm and blues. Some of his associates were Philadelphia's sound superstars / arrangers / writers / producers—Thom Bell, the late Norman Harris, Ron Kersey, the late Ronnie Baker, the late Larry Washington, and Donny Hathaway. I could go on and on, but I would never complete the biography. If you wish to know more about Leon, visit his site at http://leonmitchell.com.

Chapter 6

Jimmy Bishop

Some background history on Jimmy Bishop. Now I must warn you, you will probably read sections in this chapter that were already mentioned. However, they must be mentioned again for you to get the full drift of the story being told. I want you to feel, and visualize if you can, what The Volcanos, Harthon Records, and WDAS Gospel Queen Louise Williams felt and lived through. Keep in mind, this part of the biography will definitely get your undivided attention. As a curious reader, you're probably asking yourself, *where did this person, Jimmy Bishop, come from, and how did he manipulate so many people?* Now don't forget, The Volcanos had just completed their first recording with Jimmy Bishop, and we were performing on rock 'n' roll shows. We will continue with The Volcanos again shortly. The next part of this biography will let you see how Jimmy Bishop got his foothold in Philadelphia. No need of highlighting our good friends Weldon, Johnny, and Luther—we already covered one segment of their misfortune with Jimmy, but unfortunately, there's more to come. Shall we get started? Hold on—the ride can and will get rough.

First of all, it must be perfectly understood that Jimmy Bishop had the gift of gab, which was followed by a twisted-lip smile. Have you ever seen a person smile, and his or her lips would go to one side of their face? That was Jimmy, and he thought he was the best-looking person that ever walked the streets of Philadelphia. And as for the gift of gab, he could sell an Eskimo living in the North Pole a refrigerator, along with a block of ice.

It is alleged Jimmy Bishop came to Philadelphia with both of his feet on the ground—that's right, both of his shoes had holes in the bottom of them. He met Louise Williams of WDAS radio, who was known as the Gospel Queen of WDAS. How they met, the time and place is unknown to me. Louise Williams is one of the nicest people you would ever want to meet. Soft-spoken, and has a heart of gold. If she could help you in any way, she would. She holds an important position with the Commonwealth of Pennsylvania. And she represents all walks of life. Louise has proven she is a hard and dedicated worker. Do you know of anyone else who could do a 6 am to 9 am radio show, leave the radio station, and drive over ninety miles to her next place of employment to represent her constituents, then return home to be a mother and a loving wife? Five days in Harrisburg, PA and six days on her gospel show at WDAS radio. What a strong and dedicated woman she is.

Well, as life would have it, Jimmy Bishop, with his silky baritone voice, asked Louise for her hand in marriage and they became husband and wife. Before I write the next line you probably have already figured out what happened next. Yep, you got it. Jimmy worked his magic with Louise and landed a job at WDAS radio in broadcasting.

After getting his foot in the door, Jimmy began to excel. Louise kept her broadcasting name as Louise Williams for some time. In the public she would use Louise Williams and at other times she would introduce herself as Louise Williams-Bishop. Whatever name she used, you can rest assured it was all about business. Did she have a vision of the future? We will never know. However, the future prevailed. At times, Jimmy and Georgie would bump heads. Jimmy became hungry for power. He showed no respect for other pioneers at the WDAS radio station. Georgie would allow other pioneers to host shows at the Uptown Theatre, such as John Bandy, better known on stage as Lord Fauntleroy. John Bandy was a showman. When he appeared on the stage, he would stand on one leg and freeze. He projected a frozen bird standing on one leg. He was very funny and entertaining.

I think Georgie felt Jimmy's resentment when he allowed Lord Fauntleroy to host some shows at the Uptown Theater. To keep the peace, Georgie put on a rock 'n' roll show at the Nixon Theater and allowed Jimmy Bishop to host it. However, Jimmy didn't want part of the action; he wanted all the action. Now don't forget, Georgie came to WDAS radio in 1956, Jimmy came to WDAS in the early 60s. In 1964, my group (The Volcanos) recorded our first record, "Baby" and "Storm Warning," at Frank Virtue's recording studio. A dispute between Georgie Woods and WDAS management occurred in 1964. Georgie left WDAS and returned to WHAT. He broadcasted from WHAT radio for two years. After the assassination of Dr. Martin Luther King, Georgie felt the need to get involved and became a political activist. You don't have to be a rocket scientist to figure out what Jimmy Bishop was doing in his spare time. By the way, when all the feuding was taken place, it was a well-kept secret from the recording artists. We knew nothing about it—our job was to sing and perform.

At one of our recording sessions at Frank Virtue's recording studio, Frank introduced me to a fellow by the name of Jesse James. No, not Jesse James the outlaw, Jesse James the songwriter. Frank disclosed to me that Jesse wrote and cut a song called "The Horse." The song was performed by Cliff Nobles and Company, and recorded on Phil-L.A. of Soul, which was part of the Jamie/Guyden Record Company. The flip side of the record was entitled "Love Is All Right," also written by Jesse James. After conversing with Jesse, I introduced him to my brother Charles B. Kelly Jr., who was better known as "Turk" (that's how we will address him throughout the biography). Turk was the road manager for a group called Blue Magic.

After chatting with Jesse James, he expressed his interest in songwriting, and wanted to know if Turk and I had any songs to be recorded, or if we would be interested in writing for his company, Future Gold Records, located at 19th and Cheltenham Avenue, Philadelphia. You would never know the studio was there; it was a well-camouflaged studio. Jesse said that's where he and a few others did their writing and recording. Turk and I acknowledged the offer and set a time and date to meet.

Then Turk and I showed up at the studio, Jesse was right—the studio was well-camouflaged. And at that time, Turk and I didn't know how well-camouflaged Jesse was either. However, the inside was fabulous. The interior colors were soothing to the eyes and projected a warm feeling. Jesse later disclosed to us that "The June Tailor Dancers", out of New York, frequented the studio to rehearse and record music. (During my tenure at the studio, I never saw them.) Turk and I got busy. We would meet at the studio on Thursday and Friday nights. Our first production was an album for a group out of New York City, called "Universal Mine." Every time Jesse and his wife saw us, you would think we were crusaders that were sent to them via Jesus Christ Himself. All we heard were quotes like "The Lord must have sent you," "God bless you," "I know the Lord is smiling on you" "He has answered our prayers" … it went on and on.

We worked hard for over three months producing lyrics for the album. Well, the time came when it was completed. There were a couple of songs Turk and I knew would make the charts, or become big sellers. One of them was called "Rainy Day," and believe it or not, everyone at the studio who heard the song was in agreement that it would be a hit. Well, the time came when we had to do the paperwork—you know, writer's rights, publishing rights, etc. What happened next will show you that, yes, God was present; however, God was on our side. Little did Jesse and his spouse know I had my own publishing company, New Day Rising Productions, which was under the umbrella of BMI, located in New York City. Turk had a few things under his belt as well. I never will forget the night we met at the studio to settle up on things, when who do you think showed up as well? You guessed it: Jimmy Bishop himself. When they witnessed our BMI forms, the production was over. The album was never released. I guess

Jesse and Jimmy thought Turk and I had just got off the boat. I guess I did misjudge Jesse; he did turn out to be an outlaw.

By the calendar year 1965, Georgie Woods had returned to WDAS radio. To bring peace to the valley, Georgie decided to let Jimmy Bishop host rock 'n' roll shows at the Uptown Theater (North Philly) and the Nixon Theater (Southwest Philly). My group (The Volcanos) performed at both theaters.

During Georgie's absence from WDAS, he became smarter. Even through Jimmy Bishop was hosting the shows, behind every show billing it clearly read, "A Georgie Woods Production." Georgie was still on top of things, even though he had taken a back seat. Georgie also had all the connections when it came to booking the acts. Not able to penetrate Georgie Woods' camp, Jimmy continued upsetting the apple cart by again trying to remove Weldon McDougal III from Harthon Record Company. You see, Weldon was no dummy. He could see everything Jimmy was up to. If you remember, Jimmy was caught trying to sign up Harthon's artists. Jimmy never knew he had been caught, and Weldon never forgot it. So Weldon would sometimes question Jimmy's actions. Was Jimmy on to Weldon? Who knows. There is never a dull moment in show business.

The Harthon trio had been to hell and back with Jimmy Bishop, and Weldon wasn't going anywhere by vote or otherwise. Now, keep in mind the calendar years were rolling by, and Jimmy continued to seat more artists at his table by signing them to a record deals. Things were moving on, The Volcanos had recorded, Harthon had produced Eddie Holman, and there was a bashful and sweet young lady who always stood quietly in a corner in the recording studio, who only communicated with Jimmy Bishop. Her name, Barbara Mason. We will come back to Jimmy and Barbara in a few minutes.

Harthon Record Company had an abundance of artists. They were "The Tiffany's", "Herb Ward", and "The Larks". The Larks was Weldon's personal group. He also started and performed with groups such as the Luther Randolph and Johnny Stiles Trio, "The Twilights", "The Volcanos" Eddie Holman, Barbara Mason, Lee Garrett, and many more.

Barbara Mason

Now here it comes: Barbara Mason was under Harthon Record Company. Jimmy Bishop signed her to Jamie/Guyden Records without the permission of Harthon. Barbara was a great songwriter, most of her releases she wrote herself, and most of her backup vocals were done by Weldon McDougal, Kenny Gamble and Herb Johnson. When Barbara Mason and Weldon McDougal wrote the song "Yes I'm Ready," she and Jimmy became very close; so close that Jimmy became an adulterer. We never understood it; how did it happen? Barbara wanted a hit record. Jimmy Bishop wanted a hit record, plus. It is alleged Barbara Mason became pregnant with Jimmy's child, and Jimmy left his loving wife, Louise. Don't worry, you will witness the pay back. Louise grew stronger by way of her faith in God. She reared her children, continued with her broadcasting career and her position with the Commonwealth of Pennsylvania. To this day she is blessed, well-respected, and doing well.

As for my group (The Volcanos), we continued pushing forward in the music industry. In the latter part of 1965, we gained great recognition from our fans and from radio jocks. However, the competition was overflowing with talent. Philly was hot with new talent. We had to compete for air time with "The Delfonics","The Intruders", "Bunny Sigler", "The Ambassadors", "Eddie Holman", "The Emblems", "Brenda and The Tabulations", "Barbara Mason", "Honey and The Bees", not overlooking Motown, "Smokey Robinson and The Miracles", "The Four Tops"," The Temptations", and many more. It was a great time for the music industry. And we were glad to be part of it. The final incarnation of The Volcanos consisted of Eugene Jones (lead vocals), the late John Hart (keyboards and alto sax), Stanley Wade (vocals and bass guitar), Harold Wade (vocals and lead guitar), Stephen C. Kelly (vocals, alto sax and drums), William Luby (bass singer), and Earl Young (drums). Things started to get a little out of control. Some radio jocks threatened to stop air play of our records if we didn't show up at their record hops.

One jock I remember to this day is Hy Lit. In 1955, Hy Lit was broadcasting from WHAT radio. In 1956, Hy Lit went to 1060 WRCV radio. In 1957, he ended up at WIBG radio. WIBG was a powerhouse station. It could crank out 50,000 watts. Hy Lit was better known as Hyski. He was involved with such big acts as "The Beatles", and Elvis Presley. When he called on The Volcanos we felt honored. Hyski loved "Storm Warning" so much, he had his chauffeur drive us around to his record hops. Guess who the chauffeur was. How about a fellow named Joe Tamburia, better known to you and the public as "Butterball."

Hy Lit "Hyski"

We had a lot of fun with Butterball. One minute he would say, "We're going to the Great Northeast to a Catholic school." At the completion of the hop, it was time for another one, "Now we're going to Cherry Hill, New Jersey." We did so many hops, it was pathetic.

No record hops, no air play. We also did a lot of TV shows. However, the only jock who ever paid us for a TV appearance was Jerry Blavat, "The Geator with the Heater." Jerry paid the group's members sixty-three dollars each for singing one song. Back then, that was a nice check. And to this day Jerry Blavat hires The Volcanos, who became The Trammps, for his doo-wop shows at the Kimmel Center and the Shore Points. As our career started to grow, we began making appearances at Club Valentino's in Cherry Hill, NJ, the Cave in Cherry Hill, NJ, Mouse's at 60th and Ludlow in Philly, Uptown Theater in Philly, Apollo Theater in New York, Carr's Beach in Annapolis, Germantown Supper Club in Philly, Hershey Park in Hershey, PA, Loretta's Hi-Hat in NJ, Lehigh Valley

Jerry Blavat

College in Bethlehem, PA Scottie's Supper Club in Philly, Starlight Ball Room in Chester, PA, and the Morton Republican Club in Morton, PA. We did radio interviews in Chicago, IL, and many other locations. One of our appearances at the Apollo Theater in New York City turned out to be hell. We had to ration our food. Sometimes we would eat a can of sardines, and other times we ate biscuits and navy beans. As for the group's transportation, we had to get there the best way we could. Most of the time we utilized our own vehicles. I will never forget the time Jimmy Bishop sent the group to Chicago to be interviewed on radio shows. Besides our driver, who was recording artist Herb Ward, there were six crunched bodies in a 1963 Buick Rivera. Can you imagine what we looked and felt like once we reached our destination? Not overlooking our dress attire. The only night we were permitted to have overnight accommodations was when we were out of town doing a rock 'n' roll show at a theater. Who do you think paid for room and board? You guessed it: the group.

We began to manage ourselves; no one was around to help us. Jimmy Bishop was heavily involved in an adulterous affair with Barbara Mason and the Harthon trio was trying to get their hands around Bishop's throat. So technically, we were on our own. We were still being recognized by other performers, newspapers and big band leaders. And as of this biography, we still receive acknowledgements from fans, jocks, and writers.

With all that said and done, I think the straw that broke the camel's back was when the group received a notification from Jimmy Bishop to report to Harold Lipsius' office. It was time to receive payments of royalties. We knew we had sold over 65,000 copies of "Storm Warning" in, and around the city of Philadelphia. However, we were never informed of the amount sold elsewhere. We were so excited to hear the news. At last, our ship had come in. When we entered Harold Lipsius' office, Jimmy Bishop was seated beside him. Jimmy looked like the cat that had swallowed the bird. No conversation was struck, and Jimmy began handing us our checks, one each. Each check totaled one hundred dollars. We were floored. No conversation; you could hear a mouse taking a piss on a piece of cotton.

All of a sudden, Jimmy stood up and said, "If you don't like it get an attorney." With that statement, we knew he had stolen from us. This was the first time the members of the group felt each other's pain. We walked South on Broad Street with tears in our eyes; we were all silently crying. Jimmy Bishop orchestrated the stealing of our royalties and had the royalty books fixed and cooked. Now you see why I said he was like vapor gas, sneaky and deadly. After he cooked and fixed the books, we couldn't touch him. Besides that, we didn't have any money for a lawyer to represent us.

After that disaster, we completed our contract agreement with Arctic Records by sitting on it. We never had the opportunity to cut an album with Arctic, Harthon, or Virtue Records. However, during our tenure with Harthon, Virtue and Jamie/Guyden Records, we produced and released the following records:

Arctic 103—Baby/Make Your Move, 1964

Harthon 138— It Gotta Be A False Alarm/Moving And Grooving, 1964

Harthon 146/147—Take Me Back Again/All Shucks, 1965

Arctic 106— Storm Warning/Baby, 1965

Arctic 111—Help Wanted/Make Your Move, 1965

Arctic 115— It's Against The Laws Of Love, 1965 (B-side instrumental)

Arctic 125— Lady's Man/Help Wanted, 1966 (tracks were laid at Motown)

Arctic 128— Make Your Move/You're Number One, 1967

Virtue 2513—No Trespassing/That's How Strong My Love Is, 1967

Virtue 0000—Funky Broadway Instrumental, 1968

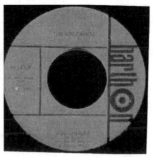

To see The Volcanos singing "Storm Warning," go to YouTube. Search "The Volcanos singing Storm Warning."

As for Jimmy Bishop, he and another partner of his cooked up a back-to-Africa scheme, and tried to rip off a group of poor blacks by taking a large sum of money from them, and never came forth with the event. However, they were caught by federal agents and sentenced to federal prison. I hope you are ready for this one: When Jimmy Bishop was released from the federal correctional facility, he became a minister in a town many miles away from Philadelphia.

Was my tenure as an entertainer overbearing? Not really. I had a lot of fun with my fans and some of my co-workers. You see, during my singing career, I was always gainfully employed. I remember the time I was assisting with an operation at Philadelphia General Hospital's operating room, in Philly. I was employed as an operating room technician trainee. During a procedure, my co-workers would induce spontaneous laughter. The surgeon would become so annoyed he would yell out "What in the Sam Hill is so funny?" One technician replied, "Last night we saw Stephen on Jerry Blavat's TV show, and now he's here with us." The surgeon's response was, "Is that right Steve?" My response was, "Yes, sir." "Congratulations, now let's focus on the patient."

To me that was an enjoyable time—I loved the people I worked with. It got even better as the days, months, and years moved forward. I always kept one foot in employment and the other in show business. Earl Young, our drummer, didn't like it—he would always say those jobs had got to go. Heck, Stanley and Harold Wade lost their jobs at the Sun Ship Building Company in Chester by missing so many days at work when we had to do shows. As for me, I took sick days, vacation time, comp time and leave without pay. I never lost a job because I had to do gigs.

This paragraph pleases me the most. In 1998, the son of Harold Lipsius, Frank Lipsius, contacted me. He wanted to know if I had an interest in cutting CDs on my group, The Volcanos. Of course my answer was yes. In the interim of our business transitions, Frank initiated royalties due to The Volcanos via Soundexchange, for records we produced. I just wish it had been done in 1965 instead of 1998. "Storm Warning" was selling well in 1965, over 65,000 alone in Philadelphia. How does the saying go? "Better late than never." For more on The Volcanos and Jamie/Guyden Records visit the following web site: www.Jamguy.com

The leader of The Volcanos, Eugene Jones took on the show name of "Gene Faith," he recorded several records with Harthon Records and with Frank Virtue on the Virtue label. His efforts were to no avail. Was it the material the writers gave him? Or was it the lack of promotion and air play for his product? One thing I know for certain, it had nothing to do with his singing.

Stephen C. Kelly

Chapter 7

The Volcanos Become The Trammps

When The Volcanos' tenure with Jimmy Bishop and Arctic Records ended, things in the music industry became dull for the group. We were so used to rehearsing and doing gigs, we became bored to death. Jack didn't let anything get in his way. He thought about enlisting in the military, however, he instead started singing with Kenny Gamble and Brooks Odell, who at the time were background singers. That's right, I mentioned Kenny Gamble. This was before Kenny started Philadelphia International Records at 309 South Broad Street in Philadelphia. Jack, Kenny, and Brooks became background singers for the late Herb Johnson. To the best of my recollection, I think they called themselves Herb Johnson and The Impacts.

Things just weren't the same without the boys of The Volcanos, so Jack enlisted in the U.S. Air Force. After several years had passed, Jack was discharged from the military. He had a peculiar way of approaching people when he saw someone he knew. He would walk up to you, do a few foot shuffles, like a dance routine, and sing out in a loud voice, "Yes It's Me." He walked and talked show business. Needless to say, when Harold and Stanley heard their cousin had been discharged from the military, they quit their jobs at the Sun Ship Building Company. Don't forget, Doc and Stan were fired from Sun Shipyard the first time, but they were rehired, and now they were out of work again. Jack had this brainstorm idea of putting The Volcanos back together. He wanted to call the group "The New Volcanos". By using the word "New" in front of the name, Bishop couldn't sue the group for using the name. (They didn't know Jimmy Bishop was doing time in a federal correctional facility.) After the three of them conversed with Earl Young, Earl located a young man he had sung with before The Volcanos ever recorded. His name was Jimmy Ellis.

As you can see, Gene and I were never thought of or contacted regarding the new plans that were being put in motion. Their actions led Gene and I to go in another direction. And there is an old saying, "What goes around comes around." Stay tuned.

In 1961, before The Volcanos formed, Earl Young, Jimmy Ellis, Val Walker, and Ralph Boston had formed a singing group called "The Cordells". They released one 45 rpm record, which never got off the ground. The group's name was changed to "The Whirlwinds" and recorded the songs "Angel Love"/"The Mountain" on Jamie/Guyden Records. It appears "The Whirlwinds" ended up being twirled—the record did nothing. In 1963, the name was changed again to "The Exceptions". At that time, you might remember Jimmy Ellis' golden voice singing "Down by the Ocean." It made a little noise during the summer season. It was a sea shore jingle. However, when Jimmy Ellis began to sing lead for The Trammps … let's just say his ship came in. We will continue with The Trammps in the next chapter.

As for Gene and I, Eugene Jones became "Gene Faith," and I remained gainfully employed with the federal government, and received many blessings, which we will discuss after Gene Faith. Gene Faith was now recording with Virtue Records, owned by Frank Virtue. I think Harthon Records had a piece of the action as well. You remember Johnny Stiles, Luther Randolph, and Weldon McDougal? Yeah, those guys. At any rate, Gene recorded approximately six songs. They were: "Your Love is Like a Merry Go Round"/"I Fell in Love With an Angel" (Virtue #2515), "Coming Home"/"Love of a Woman, Soul of a Woman" (Virtue #2508), "When My Ship Comes In"/"If You Don't Love Me, Why Don't You Leave" (Virtue #2510). As hard as Gene and the team tried, they failed: no air play and no sales. Gene later became ill. He is doing well, and is being cared for by his lovely wife Delores and their children.

As for me, well, it's a long story, but I do have time to tell it. I hadn't been aware the administrator at my work place, Mr. David Fredrick, was keeping check on me—nothing in a derogatory manner—he was interested in my extra curricular activities outside the work place. He would hear me speak of prior gigs that The Volcanos were involved in, and he became interested in the music industry. I hadn't known he was a jazz bass player. We became close, ate lunch together and discussed the business of music. When I mentioned a few gigs I had played during my tenure with The Volcanos he couldn't believe his ears. He disclosed to me his brother Ronnie was a guitarist, and he knew a few more musicians he could pull together to form a band. I really didn't feel like re-entering the music industry after what I had gone through; however, this was to be local so I gave it a try.

The band consisted of David Fredrick (bass guitar), Ronnie Fredrick (lead guitar), Gary (keyboards), Sally (vocals), and me, Stephen (drummer). We called ourselves Mirage Power Fusion. Rehearsals were held at my house every weekend. When the group became comfortable with our music, we took on a couple of college gigs.

Mirage Power Fusion

After a while, a fast transition took place, as if it were written like a play script. My late friend Sam D'Amico, who was located at 1530 Moyamensing Avenue in South Philly—where he managed five stores, all equipped with musical instruments—called me one day to have lunch with him. At our luncheon, Sam spoke to me about music and the industry. To make a long story short, he suggested I get off the drums and manage the group. He saw me as managerial material. I was in the company of a person who had been in business, at that time, for approximately twenty years, and was doing well.

Sam D'Amico

How could I not listen to him? I had a meeting with David, who I looked up to as being the leader of the band. We were in agreement with the suggestion from Sam. We located a drummer who reminded us of Lou Rawls.

His name was Howard Burton. Howard could really play his drums. Slowly the group became a jazz-fusion group. Now, I knew somebody was watching over me; I couldn't play jazz—I was an R&B drummer. One day at work, Dave called me into his office and said to me, "One day, you are going to get a record label." I looked at him, burst out laughing, and followed up with, "You must be on dog food." He response was, "Dog food, huh? We'll see."

Northbound

Management
Prettyboy Records
President
Stephen C. Kelly
(215) 247-8811

Contemporary Jazz Fusion Group

Photography
Melvin Epps

Believe it or not, approximately four months later I had this brainstorm to try to get my own record label. I was booking the group at clubs like Club Havana, located in New Hope, PA, Club Il Sol, located in Newtown, PA, etc. The next strange thing that happened was, I applied for my barcode via the Uniform Code Council. After taking the exam and paying the required fee, I received my barcode. During that process, I was filling out all kinds of forms for the record label. When I was asked to provide a name for the label, I was baffled. I was going to name it Dat Records, but it had no excitement to it. So I went to my buddy Sam—after all, he had gotten me into this mess.

When I approached Sam, he said, "Go home, I'll call you tomorrow with a name." Being a man of his word, he did just that. When I entered his store the next day, he had this big grin on his face.

He said, "Are you ready? I nodded. He replied, "Prettyboy." I almost hit the ceiling. I told Sam that if I named my record label Prettyboy, people would think I was conceited. Sam got out of his chair and said, "Come with me." We walked outside and stood in front of his store. A teenager came by eating a water ice. Sam stopped him and said, "Young man, I am going to give you three names. Tell me which one you like the best." Sam gave him the three names, and the kid replied, "Prettyboy." I told Sam that was a freak accident. Sam replied, "Really? Watch this." A lady in her mid-forties was walking down the street, Sam did the same thing, and she replied, "Prettyboy." That was all it took. Sam felt the same way I did about the label, it should be exciting. Well, needless to say, as the months progressed the group was given the name Northbound, and in 1993 the group recorded its first CD on Prettyboy Records, entitled "Feeling Kinda Mellow." The CD was distributed by Mr. Tom Kennedy, TKO distribution, 216 Busleton Pike, Churchville, PA.

On a Monday, October 27, 2008, God, in His infinite wisdom, took Sam from our midst. My friend Sam was so instrumental in my life, as well as the life of others. When he passed, council for the City of Philadelphia wrote a citation for him: "Celebrating the life and honoring the memory of Sam D'Amico."

I guess Sam was still watching over me, because things started to happen out of the blue. Prettyboy Records was beginning to receive recognition nationally. I began receiving phone calls at 3 and 4 o'clock in the morning. There's no need to mention this, but I will anyway. When those phone calls came in, I was asleep in my bed. At any rate, a lot of wannabe rappers began calling me, and I had to turn them down. Why did I turn them down? When I do a recording, I have to love what I'm doing. I have to feel comfortable with my productions. Respect plays a large part in it as well. Calling a person at that time of the morning doesn't say much for the caller.

There was another individual who was very instrumental in promoting Prettyboy Records and Northbound.

His name was Wayne D. Nance, of Jazz City. Wayne hosted his own Jazz show on cable TV. And was very instrumental in putting on jazz shows (Jazz Till Sunrise) at the African American Museum, located at 7th and Arch Streets, Philadelphia, PA.

However, I did receive a phone call from a gentleman who knew the time of day; his name was Mr. Harold Anderson. Mr. Anderson divulged to me the trouble he was having with his current record label and he wanted to know if I would record his gospel group. Well, when he told me there were forty male voices, I found it to be a great challenge. We got busy rehearsing at his church, and making the necessary arrangements for studio time. In 1999, Prettyboy Records released its first gospel album, "Storms Don't Last" by Metropolitan Male Ensemble. Distribution was handled by Universal Distributors, 2055 Richmond Street, Philadelphia, PA.

Shirley Cesar, Harold Anderson, Stephen Kelly.

The product was mixed by Al Alberts Jr. and me. The album's artwork was designed and completed by Mr. Weldon A. McDougal III. At the completion of the product, which I enjoyed producing, Metropolitan Male Ensemble went on the road promoting their gospel album. To this day, they cover churches in the South and the North. I remember Harold Anderson telling me, "Steve, you better come on and go with us you're missing some wonderful church biscuits." They appeared with such gospel greats as Shirley Cesar, The Five Blind Boys, Gospel Queen Louise Williams of WDAS, Fred Blain, Gospel Highway Eleven, and many others, not overlooking the appearances they made in the Macy's and Gimbels Thanksgiving Day parades.

Things were coming and going, and I needed someone to help me put together my lesson plans and to keep abreast of my spending. So, I hired my good and everlasting accountant friend, Mr. Felix DiPrinzio of Narberth, PA. Felix kept me on course, and made sure I didn't over-spend. I was a solo act in my record company. Let me tell you a little about my friend Felix. Felix loves to take cruises; he has taken over sixty cruises and was crowned "Colonel of the Curse Lines." This is no joke. He has his certificate hanging on the wall of his office. And his daughter Rita can attest to it; she also works in his office.

Bill Cosby, Stephen and Gwendolyn Kelly

Moving on, my life took a turn back to the jazz scene. I became very instrumental in helping my long-term friend, Mr. Leon Mitchell. You remember Leon, one of the band leaders for the Uptown Theater. Leon was rehearsing with a group of jazz musicians who called themselves the Legends of Jazz Orchestra. Leon hired me as the group's coordinator. My job was to keep the fellows looking good, and keep the sheet music intact.

Well, in 1993, as life would have it, guess who called Leon for a gig at Harrah's Casino in Atlantic City? I won't keep you in suspense; it was Mr. Bill Cosby. Mr. Cosby sent a bus to Philadelphia to pick us up. When we got to Harrah's we were given the best dressing lounge—not a dressing room, a dressing lounge. It was out of sight. Food was everywhere. If you took a piece of fruit off a dish, when you returned, the entire dish had been replaced. Top-shelf service from Mr. Cosby and the hotel.

When I was performing with The Volcanos, after each show it was customary to change into another suit or outfit.

When Mr. Cosby saw me changing my suit after each show, he changed my name from Stephen to "suit." I loved working with him, and for him as well. And I'm sure the rest of the team did, too.

Chapter 8

The Grammy Award-Winning Trammps

The Trammps

Group members, *left side, front to rear: Ed Cermanski, Stanley Wade, Rusty Stone, and Earl Young.*

Right side, front to rear: Michael Thompson, Harold Wade, Jimmy Ellis, and Robert Upchurch.

Trammps horn players, *left to right, James Dennis, Harold Watkins, and Ruben Henderson.*

As I stated in the biography of The Volcanos, some members of The Trammps were former members of The Volcanos. Former members were Harold "Doc" Wade, Stanley Wade, the late John Hart, and Earl Young.

In the calendar year of 1972 when the group became The Trammps, additional new members were added to the group. But before I hasten to disclose the entire story of The Trammps in one synopsis, allow me to temporarily retard my ego by taking a few steps back, and start at the beginning.

As a reader of The Trammps biography, it is important that you remember the titles of the following songs: "Don't Burn No Bridges," "I Feel Like I've Been Living on the Dark Side of the Moon," "Where Do We Go From Here," "Soul Searching Time," and "Pray All You Sinners."

We will re-visit the songs later in the contents of the biography.

Remember, in The Volcanos segment of the biography, you read how The Volcanos stayed together as a group and endured the good times and the bad times. Back stabbing or greed among its members didn't exist. However, the journey of The Trammps was plagued with greed, distrust, back stabbing, power play, and disrespect for humanity. After reading this segment of the biography on The Trammps, there's a possibility you will have no doubt in your mind how the group's recognition went from the Grammy Award-winning Trammps, to "Who...?" "You know, the group that sang 'Disco Inferno'..."

Before we begin, I would like to give you a refresher course. As I previously stated in The Volcanos segment of the biography, Earl Young was a homeless person when I first met him. He was residing at the Harthon Production office, which was owned by Weldon McDougal, Johnny Stiles, and Luther Randolph of Harthon Records. As the leader and organizer of The Volcanos, I brought Earl into the group as our drummer. When I leased my first apartment, at Chatem Court apartment, 49th and Locust Street, Philadelphia, I reached out to Earl and was instrumental in getting him a job at the apartment complex with accommodations in a rent-free apartment.

As you further read into the biography, you will learn why Earl Young was very selective in choosing certain former members of The Volcanos to form The Trammps. Without thinking, he totally dismantled "The Exceptions" by removing the group's lead singer, Jimmy Ellis. How does the saying go? "What goes around comes around." At this time, I think it would be appropriate to introduce one of The Trammps' songs. Let's dedicate "Don't Burn No Bridges" to Earl—and "Where Do We Go From Here" to the remaining members of "The Exceptions".

Shall we begin?

John Hart, whom from here on in the biography we will acknowledge as "Jack," was an original member of The Volcanos. When The Volcanos decided to sit on their recording contract, which was initiated by a royalty dispute with Arctic Records, Jack joined the military. When he was discharged, he came up with a brainstorm to start another singing group. Performing was still in his blood. This time, Jack wanted to call The Volcanos the New Volcanos. Jack thought by using the prefix "New" in front of Volcanos, it would quell the legal issues with using the name. The group never knew who rightfully owned the name Volcanos.

Prior to Jack entering the military, Kenny Gamble, Brooks Odell, and Jack were well-known background singers. That's right, I said Kenny Gamble. This was before Kenny Gamble started Philly International Records. Jack did studio work on the side when he was singing with the original Volcanos. Prior to Jack joining The Volcanos, the three of them sang with the late Herb Johnson. To the best of my recollection, I think they were called Herb Johnson and The Impacts.

However, Jack's suggestion proved to be to no avail. The fans and the public knew the former members of The Volcanos, and they could not accept the changes that had been made, new name and members. Some club owners declined to book the group, which resulted in fewer engagements. Well, what would Jack do next? The wind had been let out of his sails. Oh! Unbeknownst to Jack, there was a person trying to mirror his thoughts.

You remember Earl Young? Why, sure you do.

Well, Earl came up with a few ideas of his own. He called a meeting with Jack, Harold, and Stan, at his home at 19th and Gratz Street, Philadelphia. Earl persuaded the former members of the original Volcanos to sing old standard songs such as "Zing! Went the Strings of My Heart." The recording of the song with new arrangements would be a test for acceptance from the public and the radio jocks. In 1943, Judy Garland had great success with the song. Remember Eugene Jones, the former lead singer for the original Volcanos? Well, he was not selected to be a member of the group-to-be; therefore the group was without a lead singer and name.

At the time of Earl's meeting, it was unknown to Harold, Stan, and Jack that Earl was a current member of a singing group called "The Exceptions". Their hit record at the time was "Down by the Ocean." Believe it or not, Earl was the bass vocalist for the group. The lead singer for the group was Mr. Jimmy Ellis. Did you notice I addressed him as Mr. Jimmy Ellis? I found him to be a gentleman when I had the opportunity to meet him. Earl convinced Harold and Stan to take a ride with him to Atlantic City, New Jersey, to visit the Steel Pier where Jimmy Ellis was performing. This is the first time Harold and Stan would meet Jimmy Ellis.

As for Earl ...

Well at this point, I must ask you to brace yourself, and prepare for what is about to be disclosed next.

On the day Harold, Stan, and Earl arrived at Steel Pier in Atlantic City, New Jersey, Earl was scheduled to appear with "The Exceptions". When they arrived at the Pier, "The Exceptions" were on stage performing. Earl had spread himself too thin. Without thought or concern for the other members of "The Exceptions", Earl convinced Jimmy Ellis to leave "The Exceptions" and join the former members of The Volcanos. Jimmy was well aware of the legacy associated with The Volcanos. Was removing Jimmy Ellis from "The Exceptions" traumatizing to the remaining members? Surely, the remaining members must have asked themselves, "Please Tell Me Where Do We Go From Here."

Reader, may I suggest, at this time, you take your phone off the hook and prepare a little wine and cheese for yourself? For the remaining segments of this biography will have you shouting the following quotes: "What!" "No he didn't!" "No way!" "How could he?" "Why didn't they see it coming?" and probably a few choice words of your own. I guarantee it!

The newly formed group got busy with song arrangements and rehearsals. The group rehearsed "Zing! Went the Strings of My Heart." The vocalists were Jimmy Ellis (lead vocalist), Harold Wade (baritone), Stanley Wade (second tenor), John Hart (first tenor), and Earl Young (bass). The group's harmony became tight, and the lead vocalist was out of sight. It was time to record the song. Earl took the group to Sigma Sound Recording Studio, located at 12th and Race Street, Philadelphia, PA.

Sigma Sound Recording Studio has a professional track record when it comes to producing and recording artists. Sigma Sound and Philly International gave the city of Philadelphia great recognition, nationally and internationally, by way of their music. The studios recorded such artist as Patti LaBelle, Teddy Pendergrass, Billy Paul, McFadden and Whitehead, "Harold Melvin and The Blue Notes", "The Intruders", "The Delfonics", "The Stylistics", ""The O'Jays", "Bunny Sigler", and the list goes on and on.

Each studio had such extraordinary songwriters and music arrangers as Thom Bell, Linda Creed, Leon Huff, and many others. I can go on and on, but if I did, there's a possibility the biography would never be completed.

The newly formed group was without a name. However, that was short lived. The owner of Sigma Sound Recording Studio, Mr. Joe Tarsia, a few of his associates, Harry Tepet, and Earl Young named the group The Trammps. Earl, unbeknownst, to Harold, Stanley, Jimmy and Jack, belonged to a production company called BHY (Ronnie Baker, Norman Harris, Earl Young). Since Earl orchestrated The Trammps, he, without notification to the group members, registered The Trammps' name with BHY productions.

Joe Tarsia Sigma Sound Studios

I think, as a reader, you're starting to put the pieces of the puzzle together. In 1972, The Trammps recorded "Zing! Went the Strings of My Heart" on Buddah Records. The song climbed to number seventeen on the R&B charts and reached number sixty-four on the pop charts.

Left to right: Jimmy Ellis – Earl Young – Stanley Wade – Michael Thompson –Harold Wade

With beginners luck The Trammps went on to record such monster hits as

1972 Sixty Minute Man / Scrub Board—Buddah Records # 321

1973 Rubber Band / Pray All You Sinners—Buddah Records # 339

1973 Love Epidemic / I Know That Feeling—Golden Fleece Records # 3251

1974 Where Do We Go From Here / Shout—Golden Fleece Records # 3253

1974 Trusting Heart / Down Three Dark Streets—Golden Fleece Records # 3255

1974 Stop And Think / Trammps Disco Theme—Golden Fleece Records # 3257

1975 Hold Back The Night / Tom's Song—Buddah Records # 507

1975 Hooked For Life / Promo issue—Atlantic Records # 003

1975 Hooked For Life / I'm Alright—Atlantic Records # 3286

1975 That's Where Happy People Go—Atlantic Records # 3306

1976 Soul Searching Time / Love Is A Funky Thing—Atlantic Records # 3345

1976 Ninety-Nine And A Half / Can We Come Together—Atlantic Records # 3365

1977 Disco Inferno / You Touched My Hot Line—Atlantic Records # 3389

1977 I Feel Like I've Been Living On The Dark Side Of The Moon / Don't Burn No Bridges—Atlantic Records # 3403

1977 The Night The Lights Went Out / I'm So Glad You Came Along—Atlantic Records # 3442

1978 Season For Girls / Love Ain't Been Easy—Atlantic Records # 3460

1979 Soul Bones / Love Magnet—Atlantic Records # 3537

1979 More Good Times To Remember / Teaser—Atlantic Records # 3573

1980 Music Freak / V.I.P.—Atlantic Records # 3669

1981 I Don't Want To Ever Lose Your Love / Breathtaking View—Atlantic Records # 3797

The Trammps' booking engagements were done by the Universal Booking Agency, which was part-owned by one of James Brown's famous Flames. The Flames were background singers for James Brown. The Trammps' first major gig was booked at the historical Apollo Theater in New York City. Their engagements thereafter were booked in the South. Believe it or not, The Trammps became the opening act for the Godfather of Soul, James Brown. However, the Godfather of Soul didn't allow The Trammps to appear with him when he toured the Northern States. The Trammps were well-recognized by the fans and radio jocks in the North—they were hot! And James Brown was well-aware of it.

As The Trammps toured the country, Earl became impatient with the members of the group—they just weren't moving in the right direction, and he wanted to excel faster in the industry. So he took over the functions of the group. With Earl at the helm, The Trammps couldn't deal with Earl's domineering behavior. Nor could the group deal with his stage presence. During some appearances, Earl would speak to the audience via his golden microphone. Yep! I said golden microphone. When on stage, Earl did it right or he didn't do it at all. He was a classy performer.

Trammps performing at the Kimmel Center, Philadelphia, PA

Left: Stephen Kelly and Mike Natalini, drummer for The Trammps.
Right: Stephen Kelly and Jimmy Ellis, lead vocalist for The Trammps.

However, the managers of the clubs and some of the group's member's didn't see it that way.

They viewed Earl as being domineering and self-centered. Now don't forget, Earl was very instrumental in orchestrating The Trammps. Yeah! We might not have agreed with the methods he utilized, but at the conclusion of his efforts, he put together a well-orchestrated group of fellas who ended up winning a Grammy. Were the members of The Trammps jealous of Earl? Like it or not, Earl was the new boss.

Chapter 9

The Trammps' Strange Encounters

Prior to this chapter, I suggested you have some wine and cheese; hopefully you took my advice, because without a doubt, the upcoming events will surely entice you to refill your wine glass, or even have a hot cup of tea or coffee. Let it be known, this was the most challenging experience I have ever had when it comes to interviewing and compiling the history of a recording artist. My findings of The Trammps' musical tenure will convey the drama, the inappropriate behavior, the embarrassment, the damage, the bullying of group members, the uncertainty, and the sheepish manner in which The Trammps conducted their business during the calendar years of 1984 to 1997. Thirteen years of chaos. Did it hurt The Trammps' thirty-nine-year legacy? You decide.

As I disclosed prior in The Volcanos segment of the biography, in May 1972, Jimmy Ellis was the lead singer for "The Exceptions". The groups' hit record was "Down by the Ocean." Also in 1972, Jimmy was convinced by Earl Young to leave "The Exceptions"—not overlooking that Earl Young was the bass vocalist for "The Exceptions" and a member of The Volcanos at the same time. This information didn't surface until Harold Wade, Stanley Wade, and Earl Young went to Atlantic City, New Jersey, to summon Jimmy Ellis for the possibility of him becoming their new lead vocalist.

July 1975—three years later—a gentleman named Robert Upchurch joined The Trammps. Robert was appointed via the group as their secondary lead vocalist and first tenor. Prior to Robert joining The Trammps, he was a solo artist doing gigs in and around the area of Philadelphia.

Earl Young, who was the former drummer for The Volcanos, and a former member of "The Exceptions", now found himself to be the organizer and a member of The Trammps.

In June 1984, The Trammps had a guitar player named Charles Eldeby. He was a well-respected guitar player, as well as a gentleman. Well, it appears Earl Young found Charles to be a little too polite, and accused him of becoming too friendly with his lady friend, who was soon to be his wife. One day, just before The Trammps were to perform, Earl grabbed Charles by his collar, and again accused him of being too friendly with his lady friend. Charles was traumatized. Earl's unexpected attack placed enough fear and uncertainty in Charles that it caused him to resign from the group. The group's members found Earl's conduct to be appalling. Although the incident was not addressed by the group at the time of its occurrence, it was not overlooked or forgotten either.

There were two guys who were the oldest in the group, and they controlled the group's engagement contracts, as well as the payments to group members. Let's just say they were the powers that be. Wait—let's dissect this relationship a little. Let's see, Charles was traumatized, and resigned from the group. And one of the two senior members of the group rolled with the punches—or, shall we say, he accepted Earl's method of correcting Charles.

Was it because Earl was now running the show, or was he planning something for Earl in the future? Whatever the reason, in August 1984, an unforeseen omen occurred. Jack had a few questions for the powers that be. The money the group members had received was under the amount the gig had paid. The members should have received a higher pay. When Jack approached one of the senior members regarding the money shortage, a physical altercation ensued. At the time of the altercation, the second senior member watched Jack and the other member of the group assault each other. The incident was quelled by other group members. After collecting his composure, Jack quit The Trammps. Not only was the conduct of the two senior members of the group unacceptable, it was a rude awakening for Jack. It appears the two senior members were pilfering money from the group. Jack had been with The Trammps for twelve years. How long had this been going on?

***Left to right: John Heart, Stanley Wade, Stephen Kelly, Harold Wade
back stage at the Kimmel Center, Philadelphia, PA***

Remember how M.C. Hammer used to say "It's Hammer Time"? Now, it was
The Trammps' time to deal Earl Young an unexpected hand. Do you recall the
altercation between Earl Young and Charles Elderby, the guitar player? Well,
one year later, in June 1985, Earl Young was called onto the carpet by the
members of The Trammps. At that time, Earl was voted out of the group by its
members. It was also alleged by the members of The Trammps that proprietors
of clubs and theaters wanted Earl removed from the group as well. They made it
perfectly clear that if Earl wasn't removed from the group, The Trammps would
be blackballed when it came to future engagements. This stern decision was also
forwarded to The Trammps' booking agency. "Zing! Went the Strings of My
(Earl's) Heart."

What actions led to the request to remove Earl from the group? It wasn't based
solely on the Charles Elderby incident; members of The Trammps said it also
related to the manner in which Earl presented himself on stage, in front of
patrons, and to members of the group. One member of The Trammps said Earl
became so self-centered when performing with the group, you would think it
was the Earl Young Show, not The Trammps. At times when Earl would talk
on his golden mike, some club owners would flip out. Under their breaths, they
would make such remarks as "I'm paying you to sing, not to talk," "This is the
last time you'll appear here," etc. But in the end, the group was also told about
it. Oh, by the way, one of the two senior members drove a Mercedes Benz and
always had a roll of money on his person. The other senior member was more

low-key. Some things are best not said. Another one of The Trammps' songs: "Pray All You Sinners."

Now as for Earl Young and The Trammps, show business became an act of war. When Earl was voted out of the group, he began using the group's name, added a few new members, and started performing. When other original members of The Trammps got wind of Earl's actions, they filed an injunction against Earl in court. The court ruled Earl could only use the group's name if he called the group Earl Young and his Trammps. However, every six years, a member of the original Trammps was required to register the name with the Library of Congress in Washington, DC if they legally wished to continue using the name. If Earl, after the first six years, got to the Library of Congress on the first date of registration and registered the name Trammps, he could use the name for the next six years. What a mess. I know you're shaking your head and asking yourself, *why was all that necessary?* Earl started and named the group, remember! It's the old Rodney King saying, "Can't we all just get along?"

Readers, adjust your lighting; don't miss what's coming up next. When the ball Jack threw started rolling down hill, it picked up speed and landed in the lap of Charles B. Kelly Jr., a.k.a. "Turk," sound technician for The Trammps, and my oldest brother. When Turk got word members of the group were being short-changed, out of anger, he reported one of the senior members to the Internal Revenue Service (IRS) for income tax evasion. Man, did that get ugly.

Top row, left to right: Stanley Wade and Earl Young
Bottom row, left to right: Robert Upchurch, Harold Wade, and Jimmy Ellis.

Turk had not been informed that The Trammps were registered under Baker-Harris-Young Production Company (BHY), so when he rained fire on the senior member, The Trammps got burned as well. The IRS investigation opened up a large can of worms. It is alleged some members of The Trammps owed the IRS 1.3 million dollars. Home furnishings and expensive autos were confiscated from one member, and injunctions were placed against others.

Thank God I had left the group in 1971, at which time I formed my own recording company, Prettyboy Records. I retained my own personal consultant and accountant, Mr. Felix A. DiPrinzio, and his beautiful daughter, Rita M. DiPrinzio. To this day they still manage my financial endeavors. Turk's spontaneous action caused havoc on a few of the group's members. Some members had to tap out their banks accounts, and loans had to be made to loosen the grip the IRS had put on them. I think it would be appropriate to introduce another one of The Trammps' songs, "Hooked for Life."

Let's shift back to first gear for a moment. If you recall, at one time or another, Earl was homeless and so was I. We never forget were we had come from, and we sure didn't want to relive the past. The taste for success is wonderful, and is very rewarding. Were the alleged actions by Earl deemed to be managerial? If so, were his managerial skills needed to boost his Trammps onto a higher plateau in the music industry? Only Earl can answer that question. As people, we don't always see eye-to-eye; but a person who wants to excel in life, that person and that person only seeks the light at the end of the tunnel, and nothing is allowed to get in his or her way when exceling. It is also a good thing to be motivated and hungry for success, but it's not a good thing to break dishes while setting the table. The meal you are expecting may never be served.

You know The Trammps sang a song called

"I Feel Like I've Been Living on the Dark Side of the Moon." Well, once the IRS came into their lives, I believe some of the members were and forever will be "Living on the Dark Side of the Moon."

Chapter 10

The Unforeseen

In July 1988—sixteen years later—Jimmy Ellis had seen and heard enough. There was too much smoke in the kitchen. Shall we call it "Disco Inferno"?

Jimmy Ellis resigned as lead vocalist for The Trammps; it was time to lay low.

Gentleman Jim never had much to say unless it pertained to the group's music, however, he wasn't sleep walking either. He noticed two group members who always had a roll of money in their pockets, while other members barely had enough money to get by. And the two never complained about being short-changed either. How ironic.

Now, keep in mind, The Trammps had a secondary lead vocalist, Robert Upchurch; however, I guess Robert didn't fit into the click. In August 1988, Harold Wade summoned a gentleman by the name of Jimmy Williams to replace Gentleman Jim. Jimmy Williams was the former lead vocalist for a group called Double Exposure. They released a song called "Ten Percent." Sorry, I can't produce the date and label they recorded on, I never had heard of the group. Oh, well.

With the new lead vocalist, The Trammps were back in business. However, I don't think Robert was happy with the decision, nor was he happy with the way he was being treated by certain members of the group. I guess Robert said, "Zing! Went the Strings of My Heart."

Have you ever paid attention to, or overheard people when they are gossiping? If you did, you may have heard a few quotes such as "Honey Hush," "Girl, What You Talking About," "Shut Your Mouth," and so on. Well, I'm not about to shut my mouth about this. Believe it or not, the endeavor of Jimmy Williams, The

Trammps' new lead vocalist, was short lived. In June 1993, Jimmy Williams was arrested and later incarcerated for selling drugs to an undercover drug enforcement officer. Where did Harold "Old Money Bags" Wade find Jimmy Williams? I guess Jimmy Williams was a "Sixty Minute Man."

In June 1993, the group worked its magic again and located a new lead vocalist. His name, Lafayette Gamble. It appeared things had gotten back on track—well, sort of.

I think it's safe to say, at this segment of the biography, some members of The Trammps don't believe the saying, "What goes around comes around." In October 1994, Harold Wade encountered a medical condition that severely incapacitated him. He was unable to continue performing with The Trammps. Could he be one of the two senior members who seemed to always have a roll of money on his person? Let's see, which one of The Trammps' songs would be adequate for this event? How about, "Soul Searching Time"?

As a reader, can you believe the ups and downs The Trammps encountered? This biography enlightens you to those unforeseen and unheard-of events recording artists never disclose to the public, or their fans. Also, keep in mind the events mentioned in this biography do not cover or relate to the entire spectrum of recording artists. Hold on, there's more to come.

In July 1994, The Trammps' new lead vocalist, Lafayette Gamble (not related to the well-known Kenny Gamble of Philly International Records) introduced a fellow by the name of Jerry Collins to the group. Collins would be the replacement for Robert Upchurch, not as a secondary lead vocalist, but as a first or second tenor. Lafayette kept the new members coming. Another sidekick of Gamble's was Jimmy Wells. Jimmy was the replacement for Harold Wade, baritone vocalist for The Trammps.

It appears I should have invested in an ink stamp with the word "replaced" on it. As you can see, I have used the word "replaced" in this segment of the biography more than any other word. What was going on with The Trammps in the 90s? Everything that could go wrong, did go wrong. What next, you say? How about this ...

There are several members of The Trammps who haven't been discussed in this biography. One of those individuals is Harold Wade's younger brother, Stanley Wade. Believe it or not, throughout the chaos, Stanley, being the only remaining original member of The Trammps, kept the group intact. The two senior members of the group shorted Stanley of his pay, as well. In 1995, Stanley persuaded Harold to return to the group. He came up with a brilliant idea to place Harold behind a keyboard. The keyboard would act as a support for Harold and he could continue with his singing. Now there's a dedicated brother.

However, neither Stanley, nor the group's members, could foresee what was coming next.

In January 1995, Michael Thompson, The Trammps' original drummer, sustained an injury to his hand and arm by way of an auto accident. The injury permanently incapacitated Michael from playing drums for The Trammps. Well, it was time to search for a new drummer. In July 1995, Michael Natalini, a well-known rock drummer in the Philadelphia area, became the new drummer for The Trammps. Michael got busy making the transition from rock to disco, and learning The Trammps' music. Let it be known Michael Natalini is a team player, and he has a great sense of humor.

Tragedy strikes! Remember the member of the group who introduced Jerry Collins to the group? What's his name … Yeah that's it, Lafayette Gamble. Well, it turned out to be nothing but a gamble. In May 1996, Jerry Collins was arrested and later incarcerated for assaulting his spouse. He received twelve to twenty-five years in prison. The negative publicity made national and international headlines via radio and television. The incident brought The Trammps' booking engagements to a halt. Harold Wade found a way to replace Jerry Collins.

In June 1996, fellow by the name of Dave Dixon from Chester, PA, was asked by Harold Wade to join the group. Dave accepted the offer and replaced Jerry Collins. Dave would sing first and second tenor.

Changes, replacements; Lafayette Gamble had enough. In April 1997, Gamble decided he had witnessed enough turmoil within the group, and called it quits. He resigned as The Trammps' lead vocalist. Now, there's another song by The Trammps that might fit here. Let's try "Where Do We Go From Here." In May 1997, The Trammps reached out to Jimmy Ellis, former and original lead vocalist for The Trammps. Being the gentleman that he is, he gracefully accepted, and reassumed the position of lead vocalist for The Trammps. During Gentleman Jim's absence from the group, he had still been participating in the group by singing the lead vocals on eighty-five percent of The Trammps' recordings. The other fifteen percent were sung by Robert Upchurch.

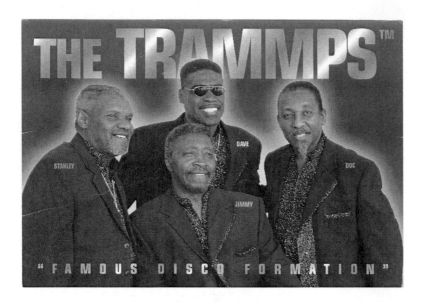

Left to right: Stanley Wade, Jimmy Ellis, Dave Dixon, Harold Wade

Traveling throughout the United States and overseas slowly takes a toll on the lives of people in show business. In July 2008, after a total of twenty-seven years as The Trammps' lead vocalist, Gentleman Jim retired. Ellis settled down with his family in Rock Hill, South Carolina, and is enjoying his retirement.

After he had been absent from The Trammps for a total of fifteen years, in August 2009, the members of the group asked Robert Upchurch if he would be interested in reassuming the position of lead vocalist for The Trammps. Having a heart of gold, and having been active in the music industry as a singer since he was twelve years old, how could he refuse? It was in his blood. With dignity and grace, Robert accepted the offer. Shall we say Robert has a "Love Epidemic" for music and a "Trusting Heart" for The Trammps?

The Trammps continued to display the magic of show business with dazzling costumes, lights, songs from the disco era, and the R&B songs of the day. Two events that are smiled upon and recognized as major accomplishments by the members of the group are when their song "Disco Inferno" was used for the soundtrack in the John Travolta movies "Saturday Night Fever," and when they won the Grammy Award in 1979 for "Disco Inferno."

The Trammps, after thirty-nine years of show business, continue to tour such regions as the United States of America, South America, Asia, and Europe. When the group was asked why they still perform, the response was, "It's in our blood, we love our fans, and it's our way of earning a living. We have cleaned out our closets, and learned from our mistakes."

A quote from Stanley Wade, an original member of The Volcanos and The Trammps: "I made my mark on this earth via the music industry. I am a recording artist, not a singer. My name and work as an artist will be forever remembered. If it wasn't for Stephen Kelly, The Volcanos and The Trammps never would have materialized."

Left to right: Stanley Wade, Robert Upchurch, Dave Dixon, Harold Wade

As for Earl Young, he continues to perform at will, using the name Earl Young and The Trammps. And he continues with the growth of his BHY Production Company.

The Trammps: Jimmy Ellis, Robert Upchurch, Harold "Doc" Wade, Stanley Wade, the late John Hart Jr., David Dixon, and Earl Young.

The Trammps Extra Studio Vocal: William Luby – bass vocalist.

The Trammps Musicians: Michael Thompson – drums; Rusty Stone – bass guitar; Sir Charles Armington – rhythm guitar; Michael Natalini – drums, Dave Rue – lead guitar; Fred Vesci – keyboards; Ed Cermanski – keyboards; Harold Watkins – trombone; Ruben Henderson – sax, James Dennis – trumpet

Studio Musicians: The late Norman Harris – guitar; the late Ronnie Baker – bass guitar; the late Larry Washington – congas; Ron Kersey – keyboards; Bruce Gray – grand piano; Michael Forman – bass guitar; Bobby Eli – guitar; Vince Montana – Salsoul Orchestra

Reader, if this biography captured your imagination, at times put you on edge, introduced to you things you never would have dreamed, and held your attention throughout, then it's fair to say, I have entertained you. Remember, "All that glitters isn't gold."

The Author, Stephen C. Kelly

Stephen Courtney Kelly

U.P.C. Manufacturer ID Number

796583